AF539610

In Character

The Portrayal of Mood in Antique Dolls

Florence Theriault

Gold Horse Publishing
Annapolis, Maryland

Dedication

Nobody makes you what you are, but if you're lucky you live in the company of people who encourage you to become what you want. Still, to George.

Acknowledgments and special thanks to the following

The Carter family and the Carter Family Trust who generously supported this project.

The friends of Louise Carter who, selflessly, made me aware of this remarkable collection of dolls.

The various museums and historical institutions who have shared this collection with doll lovers through the loan of space and resources.

Stuart Holbrook for his sensitive interpretation of In Character at numerous public lectures and appearances.

Designed by Susan Robinson

Printed in the Crown Colony of Hong Kong
ISBN 0-912823-17-8

LOUISE R. CARTER

DEDICATION

Although I have never met Louise Carter, I've felt as though I've known her for a very long time. She has come alive to me in the vivid stories told by her husband and son and in the reminiscences of other collectors. Mostly, however, I've known her because I know her collection.

This writing about another person's collection is a fairly intrusive business, not unlike a biographer rooting in someone else's diaries or private letters. For any collection, grown over a period of some time, added to, diminished, pushed in this direction, then another, becomes the mirrored soul of the person who created the collection.

Thus, the Louise Carter Collection tells us so much about the woman. An impassioned and zealous collector, she sought, always, excellence over quantity. Unafraid to stand apart from current trends, she assembled a remarkable collection of character and portrait dolls that were largely unappreciated at the time, yet today have become virtually unattainable.

The collecting spirit of Louise Carter was much like the woman. She was born in 1917 in a rural area of California. In the solitude of the country she turned to the world of dolls for company, and growing up, continued her interest. As an adult, Louise Carter seemed a symbol of the California woman: tomboyish, yet elegant; astute businesswoman, yet romantic and sentimental. In the 1930's she became an accomplished flier, learned in piloting all types of early airplanes from single engine fighters to multi-engine transports. In her later years, she served in an executive capacity in the communications business which she and her husband founded. She was active in this business until her death in the spring of 1988.

Yet, finally, it is not how Louise Carter collected, but what she collected that tells us much about her. Dolls whose faces and forms conveyed the spectrum of human experience were her quest. The elegant lady with the far-away gaze, the wrenching agony of the aged American Indian man, and the pensive children with innocent faces heightened with a glint of iron speak to us of her search for meaning in the human experience.

Her legacy is a generous one. Our entrance into her personal world is an intrusion, but one, we can hope, she would have welcomed.

Florence Theriault

August, 1991

FOREWORD

To the casual observer the doll is a mere plaything, albeit a pretty one. This diminutive model of the human form is appealing, yes, but afterall, a tidbit, a novelty, it is believed. And in the rarefied air of 20th century art circles the concept of doll as art is a notion held to be remote if not ludicrous.

This vulgarization of the doll in art circles does have historical basis. The doll is, afterall, a commercial product and a fairly cheap one, at that. With scant exceptions, it was produced in vast numbers and its most common venue has been the bazaar or, later, dime store. Few dolls were sculpted or designed by artists of rank, or, at the least, such artists have remained anonymous. Even the French, who created many of these beautiful works, categorized the doll as "bimbeloterie" or knick-knack during the late 19th century. The consumer was, afterall a child, one who could scarcely be thought of as art critic - in fact, throughout most of the 19th century, the child was hardly thought of at all.

This is, however, a fairly incomplete understanding of doll history. In actuality, dolls created in Europe during the 17th and 18th centuries were largely designed as unique works, wooden or wax sculptures in many cases, and destined for royalty, aristocracy or affluent religious cloisters. It is remarkable how many of these extant works bear detailed provenances, attesting to their importance within the family inventory or art works. It is certain that, early on, such dolls were considered art.

It was the industrialization of Europe during the 19th century that may have most contributed to the vulgarization of the doll. Mass production methods developed in Germany and later in France made possible the widespread distribution of dolls to even the humblest child. Even royalty abandoned the artist-created doll - the famous collection of the young Princess Victoria was largely comprised of mass produced wooden and paper-mache dolls from the German toy districts whose most notable features were unique costumes.

Not until the last quarter of the 19th century did anyone again consider the possibility of the doll as art form. Scrupulous readings of the literature of notable French dollmakers of the 1880's reveal their blossoming interest in the sculptural form of the doll. Yet, by and large, it was marketing, gadgetry and commercial success that remained the focus of these makers. Public and critical attention surely echoed this focus; while volumes of literature praise glorious costumes, mechanical antics and industrial innovations of the doll, there is a thundering silence regarding the doll as art. Only Jumeau's elusive references to the sculptor Carrier-Belleuse whispers at alliance with the greater art community.

Slowly, toward the end of the 19th century, this began to change. Within certain circles the sculptural form of the doll began to be considered more seriously. Profitability allowed innovation. Innovation included sculptural design. New models were created. Noted artists and sculptors were commissioned to create ever new and innovative models - and in many instances these works were no longer anonymous. Exhibitions were presented to the public. Articles began to appear in educational, art and women's magazines extolling the new art reform dolls. The popular interest in the doll as art reached its crescendo in the first two decades of the 20th century and then slowly abated.

Yet not entirely. Although, to this day, the wider art world has still refused to seriously consider the doll as art, the concept has not died. Throughout the 20th century resolute individuals have held to the idea. Some are artists who have continued to introduce splendid new models. Some, like Louise Carter, are collectors who have carefully assembled remarkable examples, often in the face of ridicule at their 'infantile interests'. A very few, myopic group that they tend to be, are museums or art critics.

It is time to correct this myopia. True, not every doll is good art. Some are downright bad, some are mediocre. Only a few can, arguably, be designated as masterpieces. The role of the doll connoisseur today must be not only to further the concept of the doll as art, but to define which dolls are artful and what the qualities are that earn them such a distinction.

What is it, the collector might well ask, that sets these few dolls aside from the ordinary? In Character proposes that it is the portrayal of character. Barely describable, ineffable, transcending mere physical beauty, but always recognizable, the art character doll is a coded message of human concerns soundlessly passed through generations - universal and timeless.

Florence Theriault

September, 1991

TABLE OF CONTENTS

ACKNOWLEDGEMENTS	*4*
DEDICATION	*5*
FOREWORD	*6*
TABLE OF CONTENTS	*9*
INTRODUCTION	*10*
CHAPTER I. The Character As Ideal	*14*
CHAPTER II. The Unacknowledged Character	*42*
CHAPTER III. The Character As Concept	*50*
CHAPTER IV. The Character Popularized	*93*
CHAPTER V. The Character As Evolution	*98*
CHAPTER VI. The Character As Personality	*109*
CHAPTER VII. An Overview	*116*
INDEX	*127*

Introduction

"....The doll, in their mind's eye and remembrance, is a person, a beloved friend, whose quality far outshines any blemish. It is character they speak of, not condition...."

It is of interest how many people, asked to describe the condition of their childhood doll, now antique and wrenchingly rag-tag, say simply, "Why, perfect, my doll is perfect." This description, seemingly ridiculous is not a lie. It is simply the fact as they see it. The scratch on the face, the shorn and matted hair, even the missing foot long ago chewed by the dog - these matter little. The doll, in their mind's eye and remembrance, is a person, a beloved friend, whose quality far outshines any blemish. It is character they speak of, not condition.

This peculiarity about dolls sets it aside from all other forms of antique collecting. There is an intimacy with the object, a sense of communion that verges on the corporeal. *As If They Might Speak*, as one author entitled a book about her dolls,[1] is a testament to this sense.

The sensitive collector experiences in dolls not only the intangible connection with the past which permeates all antiques but also a specific communion with the faces and people from his or her particular past. It is the characterization of the doll that engenders this communion.

Characterization in dolls has, historically, been a mixed bag of accident and deliberation, and, in either case, it has cohabited always with commercial necessities. Art patronage in the doll world has ever been a lonely enterprise! In Character explores the development, growth, influences and major themes of the character doll from the period 1875-1935 in France, Germany, and America. Through photographic study of over 150 dolls, the concept of characterization is examined as well.

Background

In March, 1991, an article appeared in a gift trade journal noting "not until the early 1980's did dolls that really looked like people begin to appear on the market".[2] Directing the reader's attentions to the current decade's creation of character dolls, the author blissfully swept away nearly 200 years of known doll history. In truth, characterization in dolls was aptly achieved in models dating back several centuries. Throughout the late 19th and early 20th century characterization developed into a major art movement which culminated in a turn of the century hailstorm of character doll creations never rivalled since.

"....doll history is evolutionary. Beginning and ending dates are generally not clear-cut; events and national boundaries overlap; other movements existed concurrently...."

The notion that character dolls are a new phenomenon is not the only misconception in doll history. More prevalent is the idea that the German doll art reform movement began at a specific event and time - that is, the Munich Art Fair of 1908, and that it was isolated in time and place from the continuum of doll history. In fact, a specific interest in characterization can be traced back several decades to certain French dolls; one very specific example is the 200 series marketed by Jumeau during the late 1880's while during that same period the German makers initiated programs and schools designed to encourage innovation in doll sculpture. Then, following the momentum of the German movement from 1905-1915, characterization did not end; although changing direction slightly, in a bow toward economic considerations, the emphasis upon creating dolls with realistic expressions continued.

During the years covered by In Character, 1870-1935, six specific movements concerning the development of doll characterization can be identified. It is, however, important to emphasize that doll history is evolutionary. Beginning and ending dates are generally not clear cut; events and national boundaries overlap; other movements existed concurrently.

Era One. French Dolls from the Golden Age, 1870-1899

This era can be described as 'character as ideal'. During this time French dollmakers sought the creation of dolls that personified beauty in its ideal form. Realism was sacrificed, if necessary, in the pursuit of perfection, so much, in fact, that some critics of the era argued that dolls had become too beautiful. Yet characterization was portrayed in spite of this, albeit often unconsciously. In artistry, character shone through. The bearing, the decoration, the added details such as eyes, coiffure and costume combined in various ways to produce an array of elegant ladies, sensuous or shy young women, wide-eyed and dramatic children.

This movement ended with the formation of S.F.B.J. in 1899 although its actual demise began during the late 1880's; as technical proficiency accelerated; characterization, which in these French dolls relied upon individual touches of artistry, declined.

Era Two. German Dolls from the Pre-Art Movement, 1880- 1905.

This era can be described as "the unacknowledged character". Although current doll theory holds that the German art character movement only began after the turn of the 20th century, an actual study of models produced, as well as a knowledge of German doll history, controverts this theory. Strong portrayal of mood is evident in models as early as 1880 including examples by Kestner, Kuhnlenz, Bahr and Proschild and Simon and Halbig. Yet pouty faces and ethnic designations combined in curious ways with idealistic portrayals; the German doll makers seemed torn, during this time between these character dolls and the ideal dolls such as the French dollmakers were producing.

The 'unacknowledged character' did not decline. It gained in momentum and initiative, finally emerging full bloom into the art reform movement of 1905-1915.

Era Three. German Dolls from the Art Movement, 1905-1915

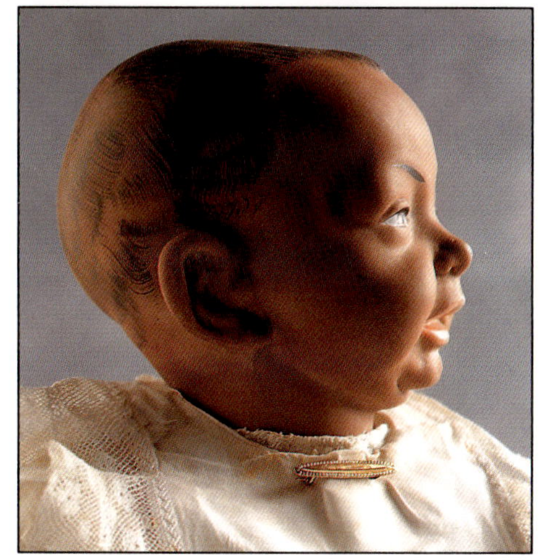

'Character as concept' is an accurate description of this era which was the historical apogee of the doll as character. The roots of the movement, labelled 'art reform' by its instigators and critics alike, had been laid during the previous two decades when doll sculptors were encouraged to develop models which actually looked like children. During the early years of the 20th century these roots were strengthened by society's new interest in childhood. A cry went out for dolls that resembled 'children of the streets'. The dollmakers responded and, in one remarkable decade, a plethora of extraordinary character dolls was produced. Pouty, pensive, wistful or laughing and mischievous, the doll had personality. The movement encompassed portraits of adults as well, while ethnicity was achieved with unique and realistically sculpted modelling rather than by simple variations in decoration. Here, also, was the introduction of an unprecedented new phenomenon: an artist signed commercial doll. The Kewpie doll by Rose O'Neill was a precursor to a movement that would continue throughout the 20th century.

A sorry combination of world events and economic considerations resulted in the downfall of the art character doll. Although production of some popular examples continued into the 1920's, virtually no new models were introduced after 1915. Yet it cannot be said that the movement ended. Rather, it dissolved and then reformed into the modified character doll of the 1920's.

Era Four. French Dolls from the Early 20th Century

The 'character popularized' best describes the French doll after the turn-of-the-century. Unlike the German character movement which slowly evolved, the French character doll emerged abruptly and its date of introduction, 1899, was specific. Of course, the French dollmakers had been aware of some time that they were competing ineffectively against the German firms, yet until the formation of S.F.B.J. in 1899 efforts to overcome this ineffectiveness had not included the introduction of character models (with the exception of the Jumeau 200 character series). How extraordinary then this rapid presentation of character children - so like the German models, laughing, pouting, fretful, thoughtful, yet with a unique style that indelibly marks them apart from their German counterparts. A peculiar and important feature of the French movement included the introduction of signed models by noted sculptors; with the exception of Rose O'Neill's Kewpie this was a 'first' in doll history and an important trend that would continue throughout the 20th century.

Like the German character movement, the impetus of the French characters was short-lived. Although production of some of the more commercially popular models continued until the 1930's, it is probable that no new models were introduced after 1915.

Era Five. German Dolls from the Post-Art Movement, 1916-1925.

The "character in evolution" most aptly describes this era. This evolution took several paths. First, models from the previous art reform movement were modified in a manner which made them more commercially successful yet still attempted to retain the realistic character look - the appearance was softened and made more 'playful' by the introduction of features such as sleeping eyes. Secondly, the classic 'dolly-face' model benefited from the introduction of character features such as lip accents or modelling definition around the eyes. Third, and most significant, was the emphasis on new models by named artists.

This concept had been introduced with Rose O'Neill's Kewpie doll in Era Three and, a few years later in Era Four, re-appeared in France in works by Marque, Poulbot and Van Rozen. Now, however, the concept was full-blown and during the 1920's a plethora of brilliant new models were presented - each uniquely designed and copyrighted by a studio artist whose name appeared on the doll. Notably, most of these models were designed by American artists - Grace Storey Putnam, Georgene Averill, Jeanne Orsini, Helen Jensen, to name a few - and their commercial success was an important underpinning in the rising strength of the American doll industry.

Although the strength of the international German doll market declined after 1930 the character doll production continued in a modified and reduced fashion.

Era Six. American Portrait Dolls, 1925-35

During this era the character doll achieved celebrity status. Although the American doll industry had gained momentum during the post-World War I era it was not until the late 1920's and 1930's that the industry really took hold worldwide. This was the result of a peculiarly American phenomenon - the celebrity doll. Although portrait dolls of particular people was not a new idea (19th century models were said to be designed after celebrities such as Jenny Lind or royalty such as Empress Eugenie, and around the turn-of-the-century, firms such as Dressel introduced portraits of military figures such as Sampson and Dewey) a new twist now developed that was peculiarly American - this was the introduction of licensing. Hereafter the inspiration of the character doll was an actual living person or a popular comic or film personality to whom a royalty fee was paid to create a doll in their likeness. Although it was the popularity of the model that ensured the commercial success of these dolls the most artful stretched beyond their particularity to portray universal themes - such portraits have become extolled for their "character" long after the original celebrity has been forgotten.

The "character as personality" movement has never declined. Throughout the 20th century it has been the lodestone of the American doll industry. Its various permutations reflected the history of the 20th century - during the World War II era, for example, portraits of famous military figures such as MacArthur, were created. Indeed, even in those examples not modelled after famous figures the designers were wont to proclaim the inspiration of their design (often a family child such as the Terri Lee doll of the 1940's and 1950's).

Review of the Eras

In Character presents two major concepts:

1. The doll is an art object worthy of consideration alongside more traditional forms of art such as sculpture and painting.

2. The doll achieves its most artful form when it vividly portrays the human character in a realistic manner.

Although, for purposes of ease, this book is divided into six eras it is emphasized that doll history can only be studied as a continuum. Movements and trends cannot be isolated geographically or by decade. Overlap and interdependence are the keystones of any successful view of doll history.

Further, movements and trends in the doll world cannot be isolated from other social and political events. In a broad sense, the development of doll concepts has been influenced by evolving ideologies such as child development or fashion. In a more specific way, developments have been influenced by money - the successful is continued; the commercial failures, however artful, decline or are modified.

"....The quality of doll art is judged by the degree that human characterization is achieved...."

Every doll is art. Good art, bad art, mediocre or masterpiece. The quality of doll art is judged by the degree that human characterization is achieved. These judgments are personal and subjective, but like critiques of any form of art, music and literature, can be guided by comparison, study and knowledge of other examples. This collection attempts to provide such a comparison and study.

1. *The title of a book written by American artist, Dewees Cochran, describing her purpose and principle in doll design. Paperweight Press, 1979.*
2. *"Prize and Dolls", by Melissa Harris, Gift Reporter, March, 1991.*

CHAPTER I.

The Character as Ideal
French Dolls from the Golden Age 1870-1899

"....good French taste has taken particular pains to reproduce the woman and child as accurately as possible, as much from the point of view of the modeling of the body as from that of the facial expression and the movement of the limbs for an almost perfect imitation of nature...." ***Conty Guide to 1878 Exposition.***

"...The child possessed an object that looked like him, yet was capable of transformation of allowing the child's mind to take flight...."
F. Theimer, ***The Bru Book.***

Illustration 1, opposite page. In France, 1870-1899, characterization in dolls was considered secondary to the creation of classic feminine beauty. Yet extraordinary examples were created whose conveyed intensity of emotion indelibly shattered the ice-like composure of the doll's perfection. The characterization was achieved, not by careful calibrations, but as a pastiche of dramatic, and often illusory, strokes.

It is commonly held theory - and generally true - that French dolls of the 1875-1899 era were more notable for beauty than for character, for idealism than for realism. Beauty, of course, was defined in a fairly rigid manner; what was fashionable, 'in good taste' at the moment, was defined as beautiful.

Yet there is a curious contradiction in this French quest for the beautiful doll. This contradiction is aptly stated in pronouncements such as Conty's (see quotation at left) which juxtaposes 'good French taste' and 'an almost perfect imitation of nature'. The French dollmakers, it would seem, saw little contradiction between ultimate feminine beauty, on the one hand, and the personification of reality, on the other. Since character or personality in women was so emphatically defined by physical appearance there could be no contradiction. Beauty - an ideal beauty - was, after all, character.

Thus, in most examples of French bebes, characterization, in our modern understanding of the word, was achieved only through decorative anomalies - a particular slant of the hand-cut eye socket, a certain lilt of the mouth corners, an emphatic definition of the cheek blush. The characterization may have been unconsciously achieved or a deliberate artistic antic.

The quest for beauty did not limit itself to the model of the face. It included, as well, the sculpture, posture and articulation of the body and even the costume and coiffure. All were important facets, it was believed, in the overall projection of the doll. Students of French dolls of this era are often astonished to learn of the complex anatomical studies that preceded precise and numerous doll designs and patents; Leon Casimir Bru's patent for a "new" child doll body noted expressly, for example, that the child's body was to be five times the length of the head whereas the adult fashion type body was seven times the length of the head.

But characterization, in the more commonly accepted sense, was also achieved in these beautiful dolls. As new facial sculptures were created - often the work of talented, albeit anonymous, artists - it came to pass that occasionally remarkable works of great characterization were among these. These models were always beautiful yet possessed a profundity that surpassed the 'good French taste' of the moment. They were, simply, good art. And like all good art of the human form they expressed character. How else to explain the extraordinary wistful portrayal of the Jumeau Triste or the sensuous and intelligent expression of the Thuillier bebe?

Although the central theme of French dolls, 1870-1899, was idealized beauty and although characterization was generally achieved only 'in spite of itself', there were also a few extravagant, most caricature-like, characters designed during this time. Notable were the two-faced bebes and poupees of Leon Casimir Bru and the 200 character series of Emile Jumeau, originally designed as automaton heads but also used for bebes.

Illustration 1.

Illustration 2.

Illustration 2. With attainment of beauty their primary motive, French dollmakers were strongly influenced by changing societal definitions of beauty. In the 1865 era, for example, French bisque dollmakers, such as Barrois, sought to achieve a robust beauty characterized by plumpness of facial structure, full and richly blushed cheeks against a wan complexion and brilliant eye color. Unsigned, French bisque poupee, attributed to Barrois, c. 1865, 15".

Illustration 3. The popularity of Empress Eugenie in Paris sparked a change in society's definition of beauty. Robust plumpness was replaced by slender form; the elongated face was softened by a less defined roundness of cheeks and chin. The highly dramatic eyes and blush of the Barrois models were rendered more realistic; over-all ivory toned complexion with subtle blushing and fawn-like eyes supplanted the fevered colors of the Barrois era. Signed "M", French bisque poupee, maker unknown, circa 1870, 15".

Illustration 4. The history of dolls is evolutionary. The French poupee or fashion lady evolved into the child doll known as 'bebe'; although the styles were seemingly antithetical, the facial model of the bebe was often, simply, a youthful version of the idealized French adult modelled poupee. In this comparison view the French poupee by Jumeau (left) is clearly seen as the predecessor of the Bebe Jumeau (right) known as the 'premiere' model. The youthful appearance of the bebe is accomplished through enlargement of facial features, most significantly the eyes; the doll as character-child, albeit idealized, is achieved. Poupee, Emile Jumeau, circa 1878, 14". Bebe, Emile Jumeau, circa 1878, 10".

Illustration 5, opposite page. The three French poupees or fashion dolls span the years 1865-1878, aptly illustrating the changing public perception of beauty. Through these changes, characterization, of a sort, is accomplished.

Illustration 3.

Illustration 4.

Illustration 5.

Leon Casimir Bru and his first successor, Henri Chevrot, were two of a small group of Parisian entrepreneurs who introduced the world to the beauty of dolls during the last quarter of the 19th century. Not artists themselves, they were fascinated by the design and construct of a doll which would accurately portray the mobile human shape. In this sense, form followed function for Bru and Chevrot. The doll must not only be beautiful, but it must be real, it must 'work', it must take human shape and allow human articulation; in his experiments with rubber, Bru even sought to simulate the tensile suppleness of human touch.

Doll lovers who have viewed the various examples of Bru bebe are often astonished to learn that, in actuality, only one basic sculptural model was used during its 25 year production. The sculptor is unknown; it was the fashion during this period to commission a work by a prominent sculptor who would remain anonymous (Carrier-Belleuse, who was commissioned by Jumeau was a significant exception to this rule). Regardless, the model was extraordinary. It evolved through four major generations of style, dozens of body variations, and yet, for most of its quarter century life, remained a timeless work of art. Decorated by anonymous artists of varying skills, there are yet few examples which do not reach out to the viewer with profound silent speech.

The bebes of the house of Leon Casimir Bru may exemplify the synthesis of beauty and character in the French bebe. Like the earlier French fashion poupees, the Bru bebe was an evolutionary form that responded to new societal definitions of beauty. Yet unlike most of those earlier poupees, the Bru bebe transcended transitory concepts of beauty. Here is the child, beautiful, idealized, even angelic, yet somehow more. Is it the sensual pouting of mouth with tiny modelled tongue about to wet the delicate lips, the slight fret achieved by prominence of brow modelling, the far-away searching of eyes, always somehow positioned in an upward glancing gaze? The Bru bebe is a masterpiece: classic beauty, artistic perfection, transcendent character.

Illustration 6. For Bru Jeune, beauty and character in a doll extended to the entire object. The modelling of the face was highly important, but the design and construct of the body equally so. Bru was virtually the only French dollmaker who constructed his bebe with a kid body; certainly Bru Jeune was the only firm to develop and transform his style. Originally designed as a shorter, squatter example of the fashion or poupee body , the Bru bebe body evolved through numerous stages and several specific patents. In this example, whose body was patented by Chevrot in 1883, the intricate internal articulation allows realistic child-like movement, yet the bisque hands are a sculptural masterpiece. Bru Jeune bisque bebe, circa 1883, 13".

llustration 7. The Bru Bebe has been variously described as sensual and dreamy. What is being described is the artfulness, the character of the bebe. Notable attributes contributing to the character-like look are the splendid depth of glass eyes, created in the manner of glass paperweights; spiral threaded irises with shaded outer rim color enhance that depth. The distinct apple-like roundness of chin lends further softness to the delicately shaded lips while an impressed dimple balances the crevice between the heart-shaped upper lip. The perfection of the Bru bebe encompassed its costume; although the dolls could be purchased nude, bebes could be adorned, as this example, in couturier designed wardrobes and wigs which further enhanced their art and character qualities. Bru Jeune bisque bebe, circa 1883, 13".

Illustration 7.

Illustration 8. The rounded plumpness of the early Gaultier bebe is clearly out-of-step with other bebes of the period, more Germanic in its kinship, retrogressively bonded with the pre- Eugenie concept of French beauty. Yet the robust healthiness has an appealing daintiness, a wispy feathering of brows, fawn-like brown eyes, palest lips with a center accent line, original soft lambswool-cap wig. F. Gaultier bisque bebe, circa 1875, 11".

Illustration 9, opposite page. Viewed from a profile angle, the bebe of Schmitt et Fils (right) and the first model bebe of Emile Jumeau (left) known as "premiere" Jumeau are virtually identical. It is evident that firms 'borrowed' the models of other firms; in another example of the works of Schmitt and Jumeau, there is a clear duplication of the pear-shaped Schmitt bebe and the Jumeau model impressed with the mark E.J.A. Yet, face forward, the dolls are unique. How does this happen? Characterization in the French bebe was achieved, not so much through variation in model, but through variations in bisque, decoration and features. Hence the premiere Jumeau is ghost-like in its whiteness, the eyes more dramatic, the spiraled irises intense, the lips barely a whisper. The Schmitt bebe is less theatrical, more realistic. More attention is paid to the modelling and decoration; the ear is clearly defined, for example, and the lashes are multi-feathered in a series of strokes rather than the more casual approach of the Jumeau. Schmitt et Fils, bisque bebe, circa 1875, 17". Emile Jumeau, bisque bebe, circa 1875, 15".

Illustration 8.

Illustration 9A.

Illustration 9A. Seen in profile, the Schmitt bebe and premiere Jumeau are virtually identical.

That characterization was achieved in the French bebe is unrefutedly proven by recognition. It is possible for the viewer to stand across the room and point out "That is a Gaultier bebe" or "That is an example of the work of Schmitt". This recognition is the more astonishing once the viewer learns that, indeed, there were very few doll firms that actually made their own doll heads and that, further, these few doll firms made doll heads for everyone else. Thus, for example, in the earlier years Barrois was a major producer of heads for himself as well as for Bru Jeune et Cie. and later, Jumeau supplied heads to numerous firms as well as producing those with his own imprint.

This concept goes further. It is not only possible to recognize the doll of a certain firm, but, also, the qualities that distinguishes that particular body of work can be identified. Thus, the Steiner bebe is seen as shy-faced and the Bru as sensual. To be sure, these characterizations are achieved with varying degrees of success, but that, then, is the very factor that distinguishes a major work of art from a minor example.

Even within the body of work of a particular firm there are variations in character portrayal. The rounded face of the first generation bebe of Bru later became elongated, curved, the nose more pertly tipped and, lo, a delicate child became a sensual child/woman. The smaller hand-cut eye sockets of the incised mark Jumeau with delicate painting of brows and lips evolved into the high intensity "tete" model Jumeau with dramatically sized eyes enhanced by lush and, nearly, exaggerated brow and lash decoration. The Gaultier bebe of the early period, with rounded face so out-of-step with other bebes of the generation, changed in character as well as quality: the gentle-faced young child, in later version, is, at best, highly theatrical, and, at worst, harsh, hard and strident.

Illustration 9.

Illustration 10.

Illustration 11.

Illustration 12.

Illustration 13.

Illustrations 10, 11, 12 on left. The bebe of Emile Jumeau varied in portrayal of character and mood during a 25 year period of production. Three examples of the tiny size 2 bebe are shown which clearly illustrate this. Above, the earliest premiere Jumeau. Center, the portrait model impressed with the letters E.J. Below, the bebe marked and known as "Tete". Clearly the size of the doll affected the technical proficiency of its decoration and neophyte collectors are often confused by glaring flaws in quality. Yet the portrayals achieved in these tiny bebes moves beyond mere technical skill. It is in their entire presentation, the deft posturing of person achievable through complete articulation of tiny bodies, and mostly the sense of command proceeding from such tiny forms that portrayal is achieved.

Illustration 13. The premiere model of Jumeau bebe clearly evolved from the Jumeau fashion poupee, as seen in Illustration 4, and was related to early bebes from other firms, as seen in Illustration 9 and 9A. Yet it is curiously unique and immediately recognizable. Some little twist of artistry makes it so. The luminous large eyes with unique spiral qualities, the tilt of the delicate lips, the style of brows. The culmination of these features convey character and mood. Emile Jumeau, impressed '2', bisque bebe, circa 1878, 10".

Illustration 14. The larger bebes of Emile Jumeau are notable for precise attention to sculptural detail. In the earlier models this is particularly true as the bisque was produced in the form of large rolled sheets which were hand-pressed into molds. The deft touch of a skilled artist could, it is obvious, achieve a uniqueness of character in each bebe. In these larger models, as well, ears were uniquely created and applied to the doll, lending them a particular realism and artistry. Complexion tones are subtle and realistic: soft rose-petal tones overall with subtle shading. The eyes, of such depth, are fluid, seemingly moving in tandem with the viewer. The bebe, in short, portrays character. Emile Jumeau, impressed mark 'Depose Jumeau', bisque bebe, circa 1878, 24".

Illustration 14.

Illustration 15. An early portrait model created by Emile Jumeau was impressed with his initial E.J., an imprint that surely signified his personal pride in the object. Ranging from tiniest size 0 to a life-size size 20, the E.J. bebe varies in portrayal from size to size and example to example. While a careful inventory of the features of these bebes indicates a uniformity of decorative style there is yet an indescribable essence clearly proclaiming that each is unique. The models shown range from size 0 to size 3. Emile Jumeau, bisque bebes, circa 1878, 10" to 13"

Illustration 16, opposite page. The bebes of Emile Jumeau were uniquely his. Unlike other French firms which commissioned heads from one firm, bodies from another, costumes from still a third, Jumeau created the entire doll in his own workshops. In particular he was concerned with the design of the body. Here, form followed function, and, it could be argued, function followed durability. Symmetry of parts, harmony of design, and above all, realism in shape and movement became by-words of his firm's works.

Illustration 15.

Illustration 16.

Illustration 17. The workshops of Emile Jumeau created the bebe in its entirety, with the exception of the glass eyes which were commissioned by a specialty glass artist. Of special note is the couturier work of the firm; in a sense, the costuming was the perfect 'frame' for a perfect piece of art. Constructed in intricate detail, of lavish laces, silks and wools, the costumes were designed to enhance the beauty of the doll, to create a harmonious whole. The costume shown is an original work from the Jumeau studio. The doll is shown in close-up on the opposite page.

Illustration 18, opposite page. At its peak, the portrait bebe by Jumeau impressed E.J. was a masterpiece of doll-making. It combined a splendid sculptural form with individuality of sculpted hand-pressed detail. Its exquisitely finished complexion, fine-sanded and re-fired to perfection, was enhanced by stunning achievements in complexion detail, each feature balancing the other in a harmonious whole. In this example, rich modelling around the mouth is balanced by an expertly set dimple in the chin. The rich brown eyes are rendered both dramatic and delicate by the addition of mauve blushed eyeshadow at the inner corners of eyes. A final delicate radiance to the complexion unifies the entire character portrayal. Emile Jumeau, impressed E.J., size 9, bisque bebe, circa 1878, 19".

Illustration 17.

Illustration 18.

Illustration 19.

Illustration 20.

Illustration 21.

Illustration 19. The spectacular quality of early Jumeau bebe eyes enhances the character portrayal of the doll. In contrast to the earlier 'premiere' model, the theatrical eyes in this example are softened by mauve eyeshadow, more prominent decoration of brows and lashes.

Illustration 20. Despite the relatively small size of the doll great attention is paid to the separate modelling and decoration of the ear.

Illustration 21. The profile view of the doll illustrates the graceful curve of the cheek, a harmonious balance to the forehead and nose shapes. Partly, the artful shape is achieved by the thinness of bisque, allowing the artist to press detail into the master-mold.

Illustration 22, opposite page. The portrait bebe of Jumeau, impressed E.J. is shown at its peak of beauty. Yet beyond the immediate, there is a deeper dimension of wonder and wistfulness. Emile Jumeau, impressed E.J., size 7, bisque bebe, circa 1878, 18" .

Illustration 22.

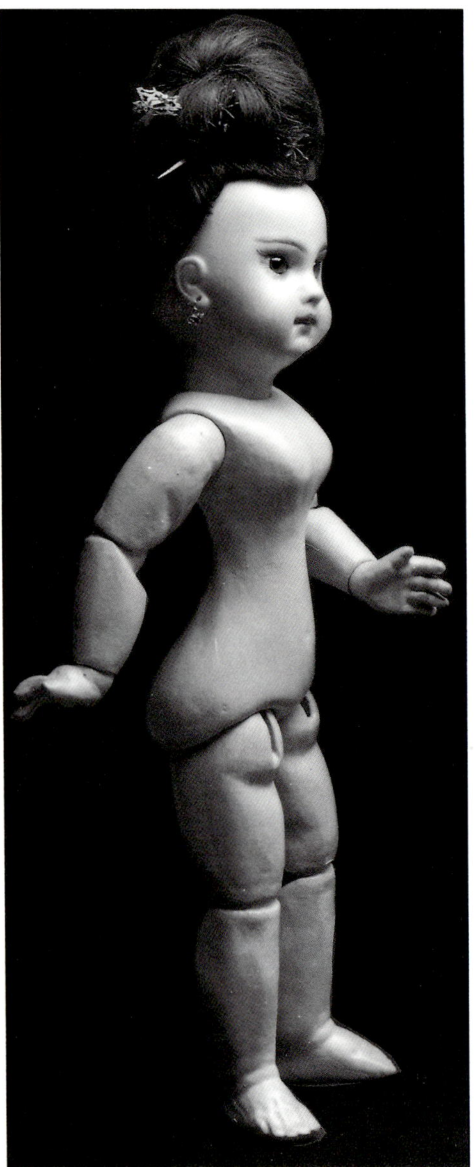

Illustration 23.

Illustration 24.

Illustrations 23, 24 (this page) and 25 (opposite page). Those who would argue in favor of "art for art's sake" would vanquish from consideration such extraordinary dolls as this portrait of an Oriental woman. For despite the splendid artistry of the doll created by Emile Jumeau, one cannot dispute the raison d'etre of its existence which was commercial. The growth of international travel during the last quarter of the 19th century and the ensuing fascination with exotic cultures had inspired an interest in related ephemera. And who were the dollmakers not to oblige?

Yet motive alone cannot deny result. And the result here is a splendid and quite rare character portrait. It is a curious mixture of East and West, a not uncommon myopic vision in all things art of that period. Oriental, but not too Oriental. Exotic, but not too exotic.

In creating his portrait, Jumeau utilized the "tete" model which was his bebe face in most common use after 1878. Yet with deft and artful strokes the model was altered; the French child became an Oriental woman. The eyecuts were angled in an upward, outward manner and then enhanced with prominent longer lashes at the outer eye corners and black, lightly feathered brows that curled upward rather than the typical downward arch. The rich amber-tinted complexion was heightened with a lustrous decorative patina. Magnificent amber eyes, chosen not only for their particular shade of color but also for their unusual pool-like depth, were complemented by a richness of lip and brow coloring. The wig, a soft ebony-black mohair, was arranged in an enhancing manner and must have been created especially for this portrait as the color was never used on other bebes. Even the body demonstrated the artist's unwillingness to compromise for the sake of economy; despite the fact that only the hands peek from beneath the elaborate costume (here, an accurate replica of the original costume) the entire body is tinted as exact color counterpart of the bisque head. That the artist intended the portrait to be a woman is evident; the adult body with shapely bosom, waist and derriere further attests to this.

The model is so rare it is likely that Jumeau created it as an exhibition model for an International Exposition of the period. Such a provenance would account for its extraordinary detail. Emile Jumeau, bisque doll, circa 1878, 20".

Illustration 25.

Illustration 26.

As the Jumeau era continued, it is commonly argued, the bebe model became more standardized. While this is basically true - the earlier pressed bisque head was now achieved by pouring the bisque in a more uniform manner, and the facial features were often created with the aid of a stencil template - it is equally true that unique characterizations continued to be created, perhaps in spite of themselves.

Illustration 26. A perfectly preserved Jumeau bebe of the 1885 era portrays personality despite her uniformity in model, decoration and costume. Yet the personality portrayed was an ideal one, the perfect little French child of the burgeoning bourgeois, the face wonderfully beautiful yet somehow barren. Professor Buree, in his Guide to the 1878 Paris Exposition described it perfectly. "The dolls are many and luxurious, but all of them - bebes, little girls, grown-up ladies, brides - exemplify this single type: the pretty doll." It was just this sense of void that the German dollmakers openly sought to fill during the art movement of the early 20th century. Emile Jumeau, bisque bebe, circa 1881, 23".

Illustration 27, opposite page. Characterization, yet, continued to be achieved by Jumeau even in the use of a same mold or model. Each of the bebes shown in this photograph is from the "tete" mold. Yet dramatic variations are achieved. These include the obvious variations of size and eye colors as well as more subtle nuances: the cut of the eye socket, the fullness of lips, the arch of the brow, the delicacy of pale blush or insouciance of dramatic color. Here, it is clear, the eye of the technician and the sense of the connoisseur can be in conflict, for it is often the less technically perfect example which speaks to the soul. Emile Jumeau, bisque bebes, circa 1880, 10" to 15".

The smaller dolls are also shown on following pages.

Illustration 27.

Illustration 28.

Illustration 28. If a doll can be viewed as a miniature human form, then the tiny size 1 bebe can be considered a miniature of a miniature. With such a perspective in mind, this portraiture is particularly compelling. Alternately, one is drawn to the fragility of the tiny object which neatly sits in the palm of a human hand or transfixed by its commanding personality. Arresting deep blue eyes with dramatically painted brows and lashes nurture this image. Emile Jumeau, bisque bebe, circa 1880, 11".

Illustration 29. A mere one size larger than Illustration 28 and surely created within a short time frame of each other, this tete bebe by Jumeau has distinct facial - and hence, character - differences. The eyecuts are fractionally smaller; the size emphasized by airier painting of lashes and deft painting of brows in a sans souci manner. The eyes, a softer, more liquid- like pale blue color artfully balance this lighter decoration. The fuller lips are more definitively outlined and, in all, the features are more closely clustered in the center of the face. Emile Jumeau, bisque bebe, circa 1880, 12".

Illustration 29.

Illustration 30. So untypical of the Tete model by Jumeau, this variation portrays most aptly a tender-hearted child. Although the idealistic portrayal is certainly evident, it varies from the Illustrations 28 and 29. Here high drama is virtually not evident, the bebe appearing simple and guileless. How is this character impression achieved? Here the eye sockets are hand- cut; smaller in size, the eyes seem more childlike. Indeed the unevenness of the socket size enhances the humanness of the doll. The wider nose bridge is more realistically child-like as are the scattered, scant, lashes and brows. Emile Jumeau, bisque bebe, circa 1880, 14".

Illustration 31. A Tete model similar to Illustration 30, yet two sizes larger, carries to further degree both artfulness and characterization. In proportion to the size of the head the eyes are even smaller, yet the ice-like deep blue color is magnetic and compelling; one is, literally, drawn into the gaze. The more graceful shaping of brows is detailed by feathered strands while the delicate lashes frame the eyes but do not command specific attention. The full lips are subtly shaded, outlined and appealingly upturned at the corners. The larger size allows detail of sculpting: the eyelids curve gracefully, the cheeks have softly developed roundness and there are well-defined creases and dimples at the corners of the mouth and above the shapely chin. The character portrays shyness coupled with dignity and intelligence. Emile Jumeau, bisque bebe, circa 1880, 15".

Illustration 30.

Illustration 31.

Illustration 32.

Illustration 32. The variations achieved by Jumeau in the tete model emphasize characterization in dolls. So different, in fact, are these bebes that it is difficult to imagine that they were created from the same mold. The wide-eyed child approaches an innocent idealism which contrasts strongly with the fevered intensity of the smaller-eye model (also shown on previous page). Both Emile Jumeau, bisque bebes, circa 1880, 14" and 15".

Illustration 33, opposite page. For Jumeau, as for other French dollmakers of the period, personality was conveyed in the over-all appearance. If clothes make the man, then costume made the doll. The pair of size 3 Jumeau bebes, Tete models, perfectly illustrate the manner in which costume could highlight and enhance other decorative variations. Emile Jumeau, bisque bebes, circa 1880, 13".

Illustration 33.

Even more than the bebes of Emile Jumeau, those of Jules Nicholas Steiner evince expressive character-like modelling. Not only were a greater number of models created, but Steiner, in addition, ensured variation with innovative artistry in complexion and blushing. Although the eyes were usually 'flat' with little paperweight effect, some models aptly expressed moods ranging from dreaminess to astonishment through the use of large round eyes that could be wide-open, closed, or half-lidded.

Illustration 34. Steiner also created the doll as ideal. The Figure A bebe most ably achieved this goal; it whispered of gentle innocence. Short fringed brows, elongated lashes at the outer eye corners and superbly modelled earlobes were characteristic of the model. Yet characterization stopped short of reality; whatever its complexion tone - Caucasian, Negroid, Oriental - the model bore the same idealized features of the upper-class 'white-world' child of the late 19th century. Jules Nicholas Steiner, circa 1889, 11" and 13".

Illustration 34.

Illustrations 35-36. It is difficult to conceive of the arduous task which the artist encountered in painting these tiny bebes of Jules Steiner - the smaller example is shown here in nearly actual size. Perhaps the closest analogy one could imagine is to compare this miniaturization with the splendid artistry of 18th and 19th century portraits on ivory. Here, attention is ministered to every detail. The wonderfully rounded facial structure is balanced by identical arch of the eye sockets. A side profile of the face reveals a harmonious curve from forehead to tip of nose. The ears, so tiny, are perfectly modelled and enhanced with realistic blushing. The decoration, while varying from the ivory toned complexion of the smaller to the rosier health of the larger, is nonetheless true-to-life in each instance. The lashes, so softly feather painted, appear as almost real. Even the gimmicky concept of lever-closing eyes is not intrusive; perfectly compatible to the doll's 'personality', the movable eyes simply aid in presenting the doll in a variety of moods. Jules Nicholas Steiner, Series C model, circa 1889, 11" and 9 ".

Illustration 36.

Illustration 35.

Despite their penchant for idealism various other French firms created bebes with character-like expressions during the last quarter of the 19th century. Certain features predominated: dramatic eyes, generally of paperweight style depth, enhanced with emphatic eyeliner, lashes and brows and, often, mauve blushed eyeshadow; and closed mouths with heart-shaped upper lip shaded from rose color at tip to deeper rose color at lips' parting and accent lines at lips' edges.

But perhaps of greater importance, though scarcely noted by today's doll lover, was the attention paid to the shape of the head. It could range from perfectly round to pear-shaped to nearly square. Its most prominent feature could be long, full cheeks lending the doll a mournful look or its delicately shaped face could rest upon a willowy elongated throat. Often framed by beautiful hair, embellished by artistic decoration, costumed in attention-demanding garb, the bebe is too seldom measured by its truest face, its basic sculptured form.

Illustration 37. Three French bebes, by different makers, demonstrate character portrayal through sculptural form. In this illustration the decoration should be considered secondary to the shape.

Illustration 38, opposite page. The same three French bebes along with a friend (shown further in Illustration 43) are wigged and costumed and their variations in complexion tones and decoration are made apparent. It becomes evident that characterization in the French bebe was achieved - often in spite of itself - in a more than able manner. While each person brings to a work of art his own subjective baggage, and while each person could surely describe the 'mood' of these bebes differently in light of that 'baggage', it cannot be denied that mood or character is present. French bisque bebes, circa 1885/90. Clockwise: Mascotte for May Freres, 17", Rabery and Delphieu, 13", mystery maker, 15", F. Gaultier, 14".

"....of greater importance was...the attention paid to the shape of the head...."

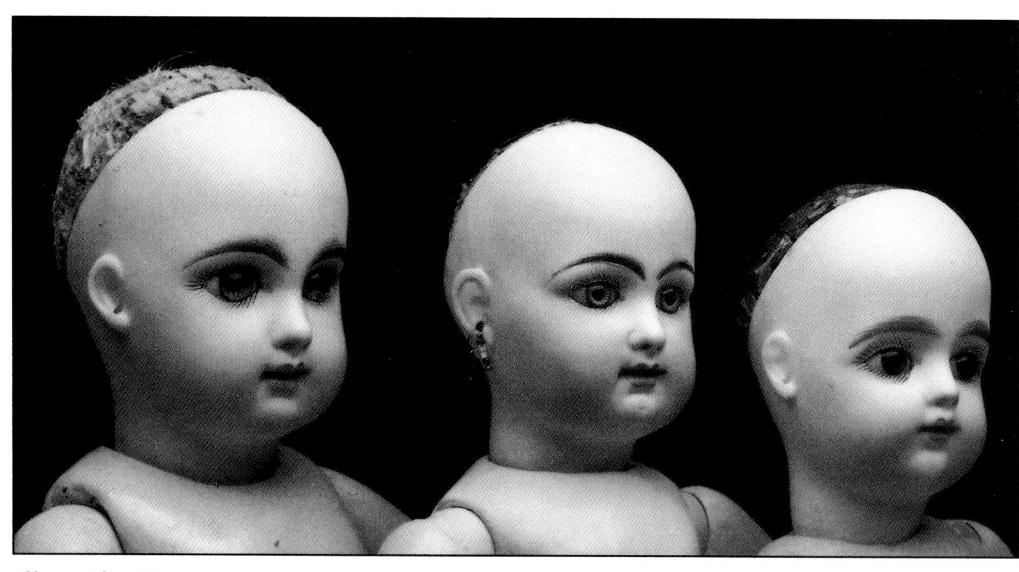

Illustration 37.

Illustration 38.

CHAPTER II.

The Unacknowledged Character German Dolls from the Pre-Art Movement, 1880-1905

The most mis-understood chapter in doll collecting may well concern the German dolls of the pre-art reform movement, 1880-1905. During this time the doll underwent remarkable transformation, evolving from the frozen-faced statuary-like china or bisque doll with sculpted hair into the remarkably child-like figure familiar to children of the next century.

To a great extent this transformation was aided by developments in the doll industry - innovations allowed the introduction of features such as glass eyes and well-articulated bodies. These features enhanced the 'characterization' of the model by lending it life-like qualities.

The late 19th century German/French connection complicates our understanding of that era even more. The French doll industry relied heavily upon the importation of German doll heads which were, then, married to French bodies, lavishly costumed and marketed as French dolls. These heads, obviously, were designed to meet a certain 'look' required by the French - idealistically beautiful - yet by slight variations in decoration could also be used to create a 'German' doll. This historical connection helps explain the great similarities in characterization between many German and French dolls of the final quarter of the 19th century.

Yet, by and large, German dolls of the 1880-1905 era are not considered to have 'character.' Character in German dolls, it is believed, began at a specific point in time - 1908 - as an isolated and unique phenomenon.

This is wrong. Simple observation tells us this is wrong. The dolls from this era are amazingly 'in character' despite their emphasis on idealistic beauty. Pensive, wistful, thoughtful, somber, intelligent-faced children. It is a short step from these pouty-faced, yet idealistic, children of the 1890's to the art reform movement of the 1910's.

Historical study also tells us this is wrong. Doll researchers, in concocting a notion that characterization in dolls began in 1908, ignore both the evolutionary course of any historical movement as well as specific facts. The most relevant specific fact concerns the School of Industry formed in Sonneberg in 1883. This School served not only as a training forum for chosen young artists, but encouraged the development and sharing of new ideas in doll design. Innovative doll concepts by these students were presented to doll manufacturers and, later, placed in archives where they were available as study models to future students and designers. In addition, students created the common exhibits of German dolls at International Exhibitions in Paris in 1889 and St. Louis in 1904. Their designs later formed the nucleus collection of the famous Toy Museum of Sonneberg which was founded in 1903, and surely must be seen as an important evolutionary link in the art character movement.

Illustration 39.

Illustration 39. Delicate amber complexion and uniquely-painted brows enhance the illusion of Oriental portrait yet the stoic composure is universal in its demeanor. Sonneberg, Germany, maker unknown, circa 1885.

Illustration 40. Many pre-art character portrayals of black children, however appealing, were, quite simply, dark-complexioned models of more typically found white-complexioned dolls. Despite the lack of realism the dolls were hauntingly beautiful, the wistful modelling of mouth emphasized by soft rose decoration. J.D. Kestner, Germany, circa 1885.

Illustration 40.

Illustration 42.

Illustration 41. In concept and development the early German doll is a fascinating cross between French and German styles. It combines the long-cheeked slender facial modelling of French bebes with the delicate eye decoration of German dolls. The closed mouth, is identifiably German in its style and modelling and the overall pensive expression is an excellent example of characterization in the German pre-art movement. Germany, attributed to Gebruder Kuhnlenz, circa 1885.

Illustration 42. A side profile view of the doll shown in Illustration 41 emphasizes the wonderfully defined facial features despite the smaller size.

Illustration 41.

Illustration 43.

Illustration 43. The connection between French and German dolls of the late 1880 decade cannot be denied, and further research will undoubtedly determine extensive cross-cultural production and marketing. It is possible that in many cases the duplicate model was being produced in both countries - a change in decoration, a minor shift in detail, and, like magic, the dramatic French bebe became the timorous German child. In this photograph a German doll is compared to the French Jumeau shown in Illustration 30. Although the actual model - the curve of the face - is nearly identical, the overall characterization varies greatly; the eyes are smaller, the mouth shape down-turned and pouty. Left, Germany, unsigned , circa 1885.

Illustration 44 (opposite page). In the pre-art movement, German doll characterization was achieved through innovative presentation of facial features. The unusual straight-line mouth sculpting with lip opening and multiple tiny teeth is a hearkening backward to various models of Jules Steiner, yet the delicate eye decoration is uniquely German in style. In its entirety, the doll evinced character; the blonde-haired all-bisque doll is known by collectors as "Wrestler" in recognition of her sturdy and well-detailed little body. The well-balanced facial features of the larger doll are particularly harmonious, yet ably avoid the vacuous look of typical dolly-faced dolls. Sonneberg bisque doll, maker unknown, circa 1885, 12". German all-bisque doll, signed 103, maker unknown, circa 1885, 9". German all-bisque doll, signed 886, by Simon and Halbig, circa 1890, 10".

Illustration 44.

Illustration 45.

Illustration 45. Plump face, smaller eyes, and tiny mouth combine to portray a timid, yet eager, young child. German bisque doll, J.D. Kestner, circa 1885, 12".

Illustration 46.

Illustration 46. The somber expression of the delicate lips is softened by well-defined corner dimples. The prominently shaped forehead lends a solidness to the rounded facial shape; the doll portrays gentleness in strength. German bisque doll, J.D. Kestner, circa 1885, 11".

Illustration 47.

Illustration 47. That characterization was achieved by German dollmakers in the latter 19th century is proven by a present-day ability to surely recognize specific models. That artistry was achieved is proven by the quality of sculpting and skillful painting. In this example, all facial features are perfectly balanced, proportional, harmonious and appealing. German bisque doll, signed 908, Simon and Halbig, circa 1890, 13".

Illustration 48 (opposite page). Profitability was always a factor in commercial doll production and, toward that end, uniformity was a constant requirement. Yet in the best of companies, diversity was achieved within the framework of uniformity and a simply modelled doll became a character portrait. Four bisque dolls of the German Kestner firm, circa 1885, vividly portray distinctive characterizations despite their familial background.

Illustration 48.

Illustration 49.

Illustration 49. The cameo face and slender, elongated throat depict an older child. Of pensive mood - the mouth is somberly set yet not rigid - the doll has bright, intelligent eyes. German all-bisque doll, circa 1885.

Illustration 50.

Illustration 50. A tiny size 0, the model is nearly identical to the dolls shown in Illustration 48. Yet her tiny size lends her a slightly quixotic expression - smug, yet not entirely aloof. German bisque doll, J.D. Kestner, circa 1885.

Illustration 51.

Illustration 51. Full body, the dolls shown in facial illustration on the left, appear more regal, elegant. Yet it is in the study of facial expression that characterization of the doll is truly most evident.

Illustration 52.

Illustration 52. In these three examples of Oriental portrait dolls of the 1885 era characterization is achieved by illusion: the tint of complexion, the wavy arch of brows, the costume. Yet the illusion is effective, characterization is achieved. In particular the salmon-kimonoed doll conveys an aura of mystery and strangeness which is not even surpassed in the proclaimed German Art Doll movement of the early 20th century. German bisque doll in orange Kimono, signed 2, 10", circa 1885. German bisque doll in red Kimono, signed 0, 10", circa 1885. German all-bisque doll signed 3, attributed to Simon and Halbig, 8" circa 1890.

The interest in exotic cultures, first evidenced in French dolls, was not neglected by German dollmakers. In initial efforts, as with the contemporary French firms, most efforts extended simply to tinting of complexion tones and an exaggeration of the eyebrow decoration. This, coupled with correct coiffure and elaborate costuming created a persuasive illusion of, in these cases, the Oriental person. Interestingly, the same model was often used to depict other exotic personages, such as the American Indian. By merely altering the complexion tint, re-directing the brow line and changing the costume, another exotic 'character' was created.

CHAPTER III.

The Character as Concept
German Dolls from the Art Movement, 1905-1915

During the initial years of the 20th century the character doll became concept. A movement was afoot that radically affected doll sculpture. Yet, although this movement so drastically changed 'the face' of doll history it did not erupt abruptly nor has it ever really ended. German doll creation during the art-reform movement, 1905-1915, was a product of evolutionary change whose roots lay in the 19th century.

Illustration 53.

Illustration 53. Model of young child from the Kammer and Reinhardt firm, circa 1910. 21", model 114, circa 1909.

The School of Industry, founded in Sonneberg in 1883, had served as both teaching and experimental foundation to creative young artists in the toy industry. The innovative designs introduced by these artists were preserved and in 1903 became the nucleus collection of the newly opened Toy Museum of Sonneberg. The influence of both the School and the Museum cannot be overlooked as major factors in the rapid development of the character doll after 1905 - the chronological and geographical coincidences are simply too strong to overlook.

Emphatically, the Germany toy and doll industry had ever been tightly compacted. Geographically, this is obvious. What has been less obvious is the constrictive, imbred, social and psychological closeness that heavily influenced every firm. Traditional methods of production and distribution circumscribed the individuality of each. The influence of the annual German Toy Fairs - now centuries old - and the International Exhibitions ensured communal movement in art trends. And even the social community abetted the sense of fraternity - doll industry families not only socialized together, but the sons and daughters married. What affected Peter affected Paul. An evolution, a change, undergone by one firm was being undergone by all, albeit variously.

What were these changes? As the 19th century progressed the image of the child evolved and along with this came an evolved sense of the child's educational and social needs. This young being was no longer seen as simply an angelic and idealized tiny edition of adulthood. The child was a real person, unique, characterized yet not fully formed, a quixotic combination of innocence and troubled imaginings. How could the community serve this new concept of the child? By creating institutions, services, and products that nourished it.

Thus came the call for 'art-reform' in dolls. Character in dolls was no longer simply to be left to artistic chance. Character became concept. [1]

Shortly after the turn of the 20th century the demand arose for dolls that represented real children. Although the movement began among the artists, by 1910 the demand had become an international movement and the compelling force in the doll industry. By 1911 even popular household magazines such as *Good Housekeeping* were writing entire articles about "Insurgents in Toyland". [2]

Specifically, the art-reform movement called for models of dolls that represented 'children of the street'. The vacuous, vacant faces of earlier idealized dolls must be replaced by models which mirrored the real soul of the child. Look at the actual children all around you, dictated the proponets of the movement, and model your dolls from them. Children are pensive, they worry, they are thoughtful, they intellectualize, they tease, they laugh, they are cruel, they are sensitive. Portray these emotions in the models you create, was the cry of the art- reform pundits.

There is a misconception that needs to be corrected here. Later 20th century doll researchers have stated that the art- reform movement began at a specific time and place - that is, the Munich Art Fair of 1908 - and was popularized through the efforts of a particular doll firm - that is, Kammer and Reinhardt in their introduction of the 100 model. This is nonsense.

The movement was evolutionary and cumulative. Its sources lay in the 19th century. Its particular emphasis occurred around the turn-of-the-century. And it sprang to full-bloom, in numerous examples and venues, nearly simultaneously, between 1905 and 1910. By 1910-11 the movement was entrenched.

A chronology of important dates of the short-lived era corroborates this new analysis. In examining these dates it is important to realize the development and production times required in the introduction of new models - it is fair to say that models introduced in any given year were under consideration or development for months or even years prior to that time.

• *In 1904 Marguerite Steiff introduced the jointed caricature doll, emphasizing a movement away from the idealized child doll.*

• *In 1904 Kathe Kruse began fabricating her dolls which were later exhibited, in 1909, at the Tietz Department Store in Berlin. By 1911 Kruse corroborated with Kammer and Reinhardt in a joint production effort of her character dolls - negotiations for this effort had taken place previously.*

• *"Since 1907 we were making character dolls after art models" proclaimed the doll firm Kley and Hahn in a 1910 advertisement.*

• *In 1908 Max Schrieber of the Tietz Department Store in Munich presented a competitive doll exhibition in which artists were asked to present designs that represented 'children of the street'. The phrase 'art doll' was used. The program earned support in the art community; noted Berlin artist Joseph Wackerle stated the dolls shown exhibited "ingenious delicacy". Great media attention was achieved by the exhibition and focused general public attention on the new movement in doll design.*

• *Although the dolls of Marion Kaulitz were initially presented in this Exhibition, articles proclaiming them "new", appeared three years later in American publications.*[3] *It is likely that, at the time, Kaulitz dolls were seen as part of the greater movement rather than as the unique inspirational fonts which later doll researchers have claimed them to be.*

• *In 1908 the German firm, Rheinische Gummi, registered a model of lady with intaglio eyes. In 1909, they registered "art head of boy" and also "art head of girl".*

• *In 1909 the Tietz Department Store presented an exhibition of art dolls at their Berlin Department Store.*

• *In 1909 the firm Kammer and Reinhardt registered the trademark 'charackterpuppe'.*

• *In 1909 the firm Kestner registered 'wunderpuppe' for a doll model with interchangeable character heads.*

• *In 1909 the Theodore Hornlein firm registered a 'character doll head'.*

• *In 1909 the firm Catterfelder Puppenfabrik registered the first of their 200 character series.*

• *In 1910 the International Exposition (World's Fair) was held at Brussels in which numerous character dolls were presented.*

• *By 1910 the following German doll firms had advertised character dolls or had registered specific designs and models in German courts: Abt and Franke; Alt, Beck and Gottschalck; Bahr and Proschild; Deuerlein; Fischer, Naumann and Company; Gebruder Heubach; Knauth; Kreutzer; Maar and Son; Armand Marseille; Carl Meyer; Nockler and Tittel; Porzellanfabrik Rauenstein; Max Rader; Paul Rauschert; Gustav Schmey; Bruno Schmidt; Franz Schmidt, George Schmidt, Swaine and Company and Wislizenus. Not only were the firms specific in description of the doll's character portrayal in court filings, but their advertisements of the period are rife with terminology of the movement: Nockler and Tittel noted their "reform dolls, art dolls" and Gustav Schmey offered "great choice in character dolls".*

By 1911 the character art-reform movement was well entrenched although now manufacturers had begun to question its commercial success. The start-up cost of the plethora of new models was costly, the actual manufacturing cost was high as well, and the popularity of the dolls for the average consumer was less than hoped. Although new models continued to be introduced until 1915 the initial enthusiasm became dampened. World War I dampened the enthusiasm further and it is fair to say that after the war the movement, in its purest sense, was abandoned.

Yet not entirely. Although no new models were introduced the firms continued their production of designs that had enjoyed commercial popularity. Further, the idea of deliberately wrought characterization in dolls was not abandoned. Instead the idea continued its evolution and was transformed again into the compromised character doll of the 1920's.

The Character as Concept art-reform movement of 1905-1915 was of short duration yet its influence was of the highest magnitude. During that short ten year span an amazing number and variety of outstanding doll models was conceived and created. The concept continues to influence the doll artist of today.

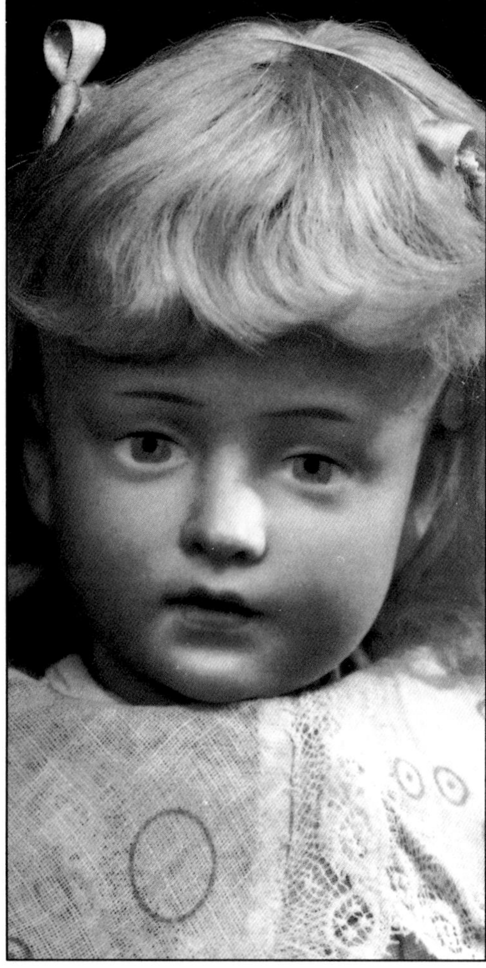

Illustration 54.

Illustration 54. Model of young child from the Simon and Halbig firm, circa 1910. 13", model 150, circa 1910.

1. Design in dolls was not isolated from other artistic movements of the time. The American artist Thomas Eakin's 'oiil painting Portrait of Master Douty', painted in 1906, as one example, is remarkably similar in character and style to the doll portrayal of this era.

2. "Insurgents in Toyland", Eva Elise Vom Baur, Good Housekeeping Magazine, December 1911, page 739 proclaimed "Toyland has been undergoing a revolution" in her examination of the new concept dolls by Kathe Kruse.

3. "New German Dollies with Personality", The Craftsman, December, 1911, page 334.

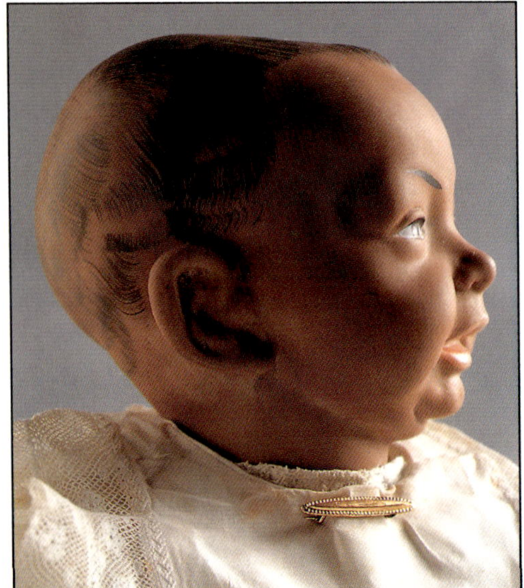

Illustration 55.

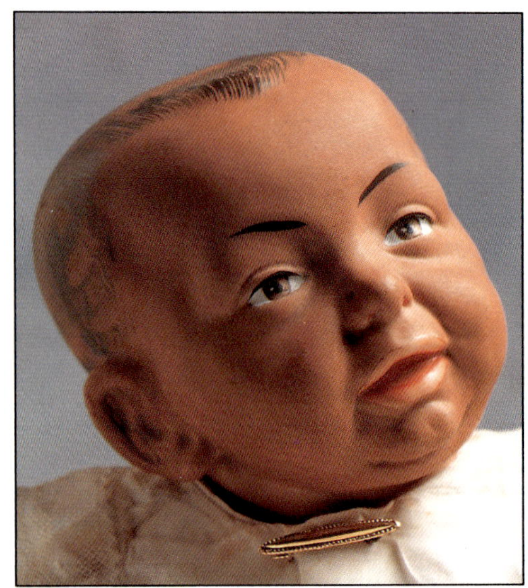

Illustration 56.

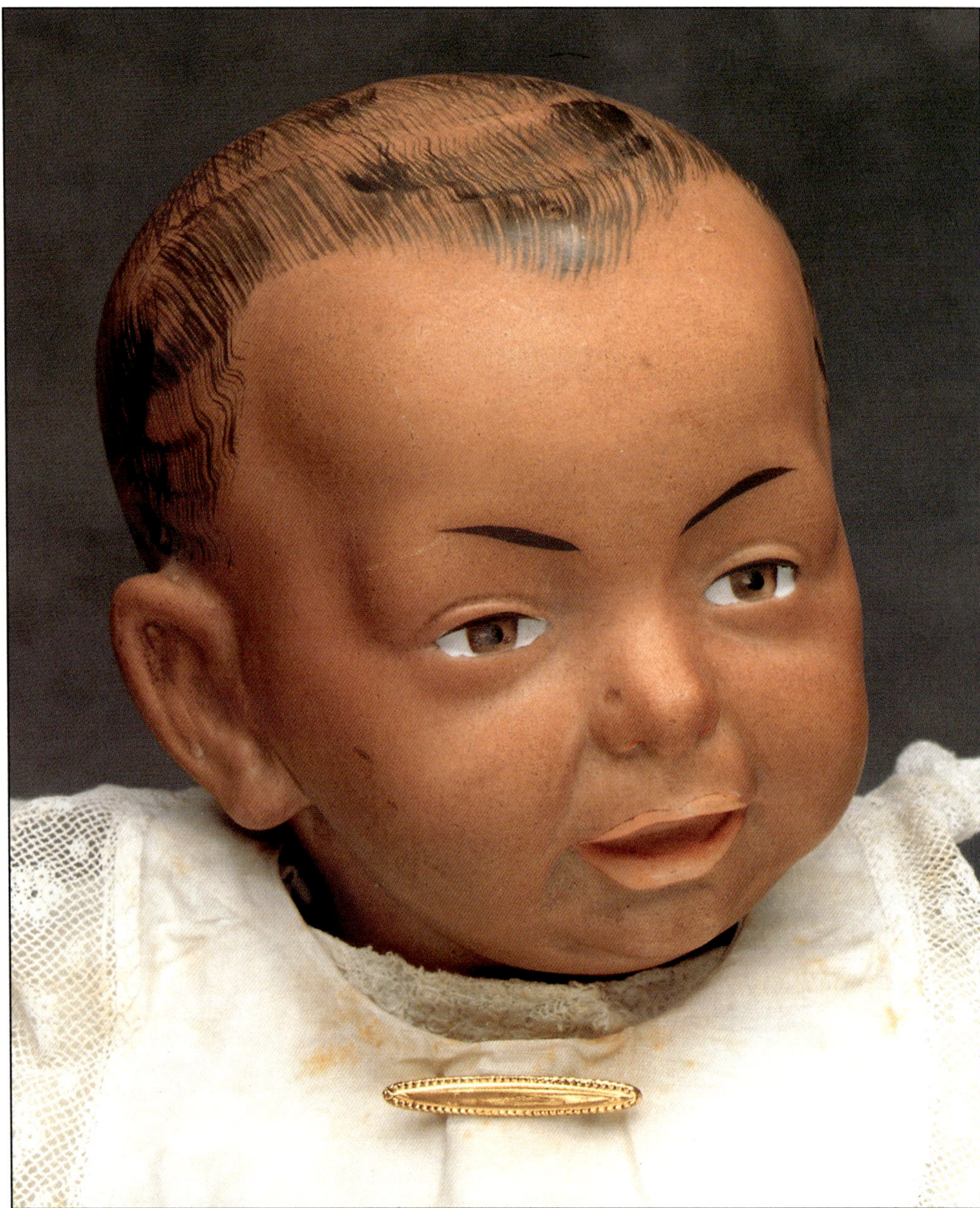

Illustration 57.

Illustrations 55, 56, 57. The facial structure of this young child was a shocking departure from conventional doll models of the era. Labelled "our famous baby head" by Kammer and Reinhardt, it waś, in fact, the first model from their 1909 newly trademarked "Charackterpuppe" series. The realistic portrayal was accomplished by definition of the fragile baby skull, impressed temples, rounded and upturned nose, abundance of dimples and detailed sculpting around the mouth and chin. The original model portrayed a white child, but the model also appeared with brown or black complexion; interestingly, the model works effectively with each complexion tone. Seen in various perspectives, the detailed modelling creates a truly life-like impression. Kammer and Reinhardt, model 100, 16", 1909.

Illustration 58, opposite page. During 1909 and 1910 several other models were introduced by Kammer and Reinhardt. Designed by sculptor Karl Krausser after actual children (including the grandchild of Franz Reinhardt) the dolls can truly be described as 'children of the streets' as called for in the Munich Art Fair creed of 1908. The brown-eyed model depicts an older child with slender face and fuller lips in contrast to the round-faced modelling of the blue- eyed child. In both examples, the characterization is achieved through subtlety of sculpting and deceivingly simple decoration. Unlike the elaborately feathered brows of French bebes, for example, the brow of the Kammer and Reinhardt child is a simple, single stroke. So mournful, so plaintive is their expression that one wonders if they have a prescient vision of the soon-to- come world turbulence. Kammer and Reinhardt, models 109 and 114, circa 1909.

Illustration 58.

Illustration 59.

Illustration 59. Kammer and Reinhardt's model 109 shown in 3/4 profile. Her sculpted detail is well-delineated, circa 1910, 14".

Illustration 60..

Illustration 60. So much alike, yet so different. Kammer and Reinhardt's 114 model has wonderfully defined bone structure, circa 1910, 15".

Illustration 61.

Illustration 61. The second model from the Kammer and Reinhardt character series, 101, depicted a pouty-faced child. A sorrowful expression is accomplished, not only through modelling of the downcast mouth, but from the far-away gaze in the heavily-lidded eyes. Glancing just slightly to the side, the eyes have decorative glaze that hints at tearfulness. The powdery-like complexion is a distinctive quality of the Kammer and Reinhardt character dolls. The larger model, 21", contrasts a tiny 8" example, illuminating the superlative sculpting of this character series. Kammer and Reinhardt, models 101, circa 1909.

Illustration 62.

Illustration 62. Despite the apparent simplicity of decoration in the Kammer and Reinhardt character series, it is evident that this is only a delusion. How else, one asks, could such individual expression be achieved within the same model? The compelling brown eyes of the larger doll soften her fevered blush and dominate her two shy-eyed companions. The smaller blue-eyed child is an identical model yet the appearance is amazingly varied. Kammer and Reinhardt, models 101 and 114, 8"-10", circa 1909.

Illustration 63-67. A gentle and knowing sadness pervades this portrait of an adult woman. Her turn-of-the-century origin is evident in costume, yet her portraiture is timeless.

How is this character achieved? All seems simplicity itself, smooth lines, uncluttered decoration. Yet it is through this very simplicity that character is deeded. The strong planes of facial structure terminating in high forehead, the firm set of the jawline softened by elegantly pointed chin, the aquiline nose balanced by softly impressed temples are subtle, unobtrusive yet magnificent in their overall effect. In particular, however, it is the presence of the eyes that is compelling. The lids are half-closed in a dreamy manner that casts her gaze downward. The eyes themselves are concave rather than simple flat plane, and that curve lends a splendid depth to the eye. What is not evident is the sculpting exposed when the doll is held, wigless, to the light; here the various thicknesses of the bisque are exposed. It becomes evident that the very thinness of bisque and delicacy of modelling around the eyes is an effective counterpoint to the thickness - and firmness - of the jawline - a deliberate sculpting device employed by the artist.

Particularly unusual about this model is the certainty of its gender. Body modelling aside, the figure is definitively feminine. Decoration nurtures this image in the rich roundness of lips, for example, yet it is difficult to conceive that the basic sculpture itself could be decorated in a manner that would override the suggestion of female. Simon and Halbig, model 152, 22", circa 1910.

Illustration 63.

Illustration 64.

Illustration 65.

Illustration 66.

Illustration 67.

Illustration 68, 69, 70. A further model from the Simon and Halbig character series is notable for the angularity of facial structure. The fullness of crown and penetrating gaze of upper glancing eyes convey a potent intelligence softened by sensitivity. A full-front view of the head suggests nearly flat facial planes; only when the head is angled is the detail of rich sculpting elaborated. Simon and Halbig, model 150, 15", circa 1910.

Illustration 68.

Illustration 69.

Illustration 70.

Illustration 71.

Illustration 71. The mirthful expression of this character child is a harmonious blend of sculpting and decorative technique. The upper-glancing eyes are widened, dimples are sculpted into the cheeks and around the mouth and the lips are painted in the most tentative of smiles. To understand how subtle, yet synergetic, is this mood portrayal one should examine the doll, feature by feature. Cover first the eyes, alternately the cheeks, then the mouth. In each instance, it is obvious that the portrayal relies upon total presentation; any one aspect being absent dramatically alters the overall characterization. Simon and Halbig, model 151, 14", circa 1910.

Illustration 72. Models - sometimes exactly, sometimes in variation - were freely 'borrowed' from one firm by another during the short-lived art-character movement. In this instance, the Simon and Halbig model shown in Illustration 71 is compared to variations of the model produced, concurrently, by the Kestner firm. In fact, so nearly identical are the models, that any differences can be explained by the suggested age difference of the portrayed child; the Kestner models appears to be younger sibling of the slightly more angular Simon and Halbig child. Further examples of the Kestner children are shown in Illustration 74.

Illustration 72.

Illustration 73.

Illustration 73. Many firms participated in the art character movement. Hence collectors who pride themselves on ready visual identification of facial models are often surprised at curiosities that appear. This model, for instance, which bears the double indicia of Bahr and Proschild and Swaine and Company, is a surprising departure. And despite tiny size the characterization is well-detailed in sculpting and decorative technique. Bahr and Proschild for Swaine and Company, 10", circa 1912.

Illustration 74. Three models from the Kestner 180 series are compared. The larger model, with no impressed model number, appears to be the duplicate model of the blue-eyed child; only variations in decoration of mouth and larger eyes account for the uniqueness of presence. The eyes are larger and upper-gazing in the larger model, for instance, while in the smaller doll the eyes are tiny and tease slightly sideways. Both examples are adorned with a unique painting of upper lashes: a bouquet spray centered on the black painted eyeliner. Although the eyes are burnished with a lustrous glaze the planes of the eyes are flat, unlike the character models shown previously by Simon and Halbig. The glass-eyed child has a softer, more realistic expression; emphasized curling lashes completely encircle the eye. Kestner, the two smaller models impressed 185, 12", 13", 16". circa 1910.

Illustration 74.

Illustration 75.

Illustrations 75-76. Fascination with exotic cultures included the American Indian. An extraordinary model by Gebruder Heubach is worthy of the masterpiece designation. Devoid of sentimentality, stripped of cliche, the model is universal and timeless in its portrayal. The taut leathered face is weary, the cheeks sunken, the flesh thinned to the bone. No noble savage is this, no fierce warrior. Simply an old man, tired, worn, yet still imbued with dignity. One is reminded of the period photographs of Edward Curtis. This characterization is all the more remarkable given the popularity of the Wild West shows in Europe at that time and the resultant stereotypical view of the American Indian. Gebruder Heubach, model 9467, 14", circa 1910.

The dolls of Gebruder Heubach may represent the apogee of the art character movement in Germany. Representative of the era in their projection of 'children of the street', the dolls are, nonetheless, unique in stylistic techniques. In the earlier models, for example, the sense of hand-pressed sculpting is omnipresent. So pervasively realistic is the complexion texture, the tousled coiffure, the gaze of the eyes that were it not for the tattle-tale seamlines at the sides of the head one could believe each model was uniquely sculpted. This uniqueness is the result of two historical factors. First was transition within the company. Originally a producer of household goods, then knick-knacks, and then finally, toward the end of the 19th century, of ornamental sculpture - most notably of children - the company made a natural progression to the production of dolls, and these dolls, naturally, resembled their statuary progenitors. Secondly was the close working relationship with the school for sculptors in Lichte. Heubach had developed a connection with this school as early as its founding in 1862 and the Lichte sculptors were responsible for the design and creation of most of the noted Heubach figurines, and later, its dolls. The connection with Lichte may have been unique among German dollmakers and helps explain the unique nature of these dolls.

Illustration 76.

Illustrations 77, 78, 80. One could be convinced that a sculptor modelled this specific work, hand-pressing the multitude of details and facial planes, detailing each curl with hand-worked artist implements. Yet the seam lines at the sides of the head belie this impression; the doll was made in mold. One wonders simultaneously how was this possible and why wasn't it always?

The head is magnificent. There is no compromise here with a simply impressed dimple, an accurately-placed accent line. The entire face is a study in motion - kinetic, alive, exuberant. Other character doll makers relied upon design, decoration and finish to convey a concept. In the early Heubach models a fourth dimension was added: texture. Close your eyes, feel the face, compare it to another character (even a slightly later example by Heubach): the textural differences are remarkable. It is this texture that gives to the early Heubach character dolls their incomparable artistry. Gebruder Heubach, model 7764, 17", circa 1910.

Illustration 79. In this comparison example with a slightly later Heubach character the textural differences are obvious. Although the blue-ribboned girl is lovely, a study in mis-placed demureness, (the eyes, in particular, appearing so realistic), yet she is listless in the company of the pink-ribboned girl. Gebruder Heubach, model 7853, 14", circa 1910-1915.

Illustration 77.

Illustration 78.

Illustration 79.

Illustration 80.

Illustrations 81, 82, 83. Two additional early models by Gebruder Heubach convey the fourth dimension of textural definition. Texture brings energy to the sculptural form, and the dolls are no exception. They seem to be always in motion, their faces alive.

The detail of characterization in the Heubach dolls extended completely around the head. Each boy has a well-detailed toddler fat roll at the nape of neck. Both by Gebruder Heubach; crying boy, model 7761, 19", circa 1910; adoring boy, model 7743, 17", circa 1909.

Illustration 81.

Illustration 82.

Illustration 83.

Illustration 84. Although produced only two or three years later, these models by Gebruder Heubach lack the textural dimension of the three previous models. Nonetheless their characterization is enchanting and various moods of "children in the street" are artfully portrayed. In these Heubach models, it could be said, the eyes are the mirror of the soul; it is notable that the eyes retain the textural dimension of the previously shown models. This sculptural depth of eyes is referred to as 'intaglio' by collectors and it is made more prominent by enlarged size of black pupil and applied white 'bead' eye dot. In the smiling model, the bead technique is also used to create lower teeth; it is a well-chosen technique for the teeth are so delicate as to accurately suggest newly-grown baby teeth.

These three faces all appear on Heubach all-bisque figurines of the same period. Further, variations were possible in other dolls; some were created as wigged models, and, only slightly later, the smiling facial mold was made with glass sleep eyes.

All by Gebruder Heubach, circa 1912; smiling model, 16"; somber model 7622, 14", grinning model 7811, 14".

Illustration 84.

Illustration 85.

Illustration 85. An interesting offshoot of the character movement was the use of character heads in novelty objects. Bisque dolls had traditionally been used in the production of related items: automata, party favors, boudoir objects, even as the 'head' of a purse or sewing bag. This use continued during the character doll era and had two variations: the use of portrait heads designed to actually resemble an historical or famous figure; and the use of caricature funny-faced figures. The first variation is illustrated in the portrait of George Washington on a horse; the body of the horse is actually a candy container. Although the portraiture certainly resembles Washington there is little doubt that the original presentation and costume aid in this enactment. The second variation is shown in the funny-faced soldiers, whose bodies, also, form a candy container. The modelling appears to be unique in this case, and, despite its exaggerated qualities, is immensely appealing, 14" and 11", circa 1910.

Illustration 86. In a nod to popular appeal the painted eye doll soon evolved into character faces designed with sleeping glass eyes. With this compromise the doll firms hoped to continue the thrust of the art movement - to create real 'children of the streets' - yet gain a popularity that would make their production commercially feasible. Kammer and Reinhardt, quick to initiate the art doll movement, was also quick to introduce the change. In 1911 - just two years later - they introduced the character model, 115A, with sleeping eyes. The wonderfully-sculptured features still remained - hollowed impressions around the eyes, plumply modelled lower face with delineated chin, slightly over- sized ears, and downcast lips (achieved more through decoration than actually modelling) - yet the use of glass eyes seemed to make the object more alive, less a sculpture. Kammer and Reinhardt, model 115A, 15", circa 1911.

Illustration 87. Doll firms continued to 'borrow' freely from each other in concept and, sometimes, in actual design. In reality, the firms copied, not so much from each other, as from Renaissance models of the 17th century which were currently in vogue in Europe. Thus the 115A model of Kammer and Reinhardt is remarkably similar to Fany by Armand Marseille, as well as the first model of the cloth doll maker Kathe Kruse. In actuality all three were based on a 17th century sculpture by Francois du Quesnoy. Armand Marseille, model 231 Fany, 14", circa 1911 and Kammer and Reinhardt listed above.

Illustration 86.

Illustration 87.

Illustration 88.

Illustration 88. An exaggeration of features characterized many models of the art movement. The designers, in their quest to portray 'children of the streets,' walked a very delicate path between caricature and sentimentality. The success of the doll depended, then, upon the quality of decoration to soften the caricature, to individualize the sentimental. Two examples illustrate this point; it is the able use of decorative techniques that enhances them. The model with tiny eyes verges upon caricature with his under-sized eyes and crooked smile, yet the judicious choice of subtle decoration of brows and lashes along with beautifully shaded lips softens this impression. Simon and Halbig, model 1428, 15", circa 1912. Kammer and Reinhardt, model 116, 14" circa 1912.

Illustration 89.

Illustration 89. A 3/4 profile view of the same dolls shows varying degree of sculpting detail and technique.

Illustration 90.

Illustration 90. By 1912 the Kammer and Reinhardt firm had introduced the 121 model. Little unique characterization of face remained and from here it was but a short step to the 'dolly- faced characters' described in Chapter V. Here the portrayal is achieved through the basic shape of the rounded face and through exaggerated painting of brows and lashes. Kammer and Reinhardt, model 121, 13", circa 1912.

Illustration 91. Kammer and Reinhardt's model 117, known as Mein Liebling, was a culmination of the union of character and commercial success. The wistful child depicted in the 101 and 114 models is enlivened by large rounded glass eyes. The mouth, smaller, is more delicate. Here is an idealistic image of childhood, yet rendered tender, intelligent, real. The model was only fully perfected in larger examples; as the mold was 'shrunk' in the creation of smaller sizes it lost much of its definition. Especially intriguing in a comparison of 117 models is the patina; some models bear a very lustrous, gleaming complexion while others are soft and powder-like. This seemingly simple variation creates a dramatic change in their portrayal. Kammer and Reinhardt, model 117, 11", circa 1912.

Illustration 91.

Illustration 92, opposite page. In a few examples, the glass-eyed character dolls projected the dramatic essence of the painted eye series. This is one example. Marked only 111, the doll is believed to be an early series created by Simon and Halbig. The characterization - thoughtful, sensitive, wistful - is achieved not so much through subtleties of modelling as through decorative techniques. The firm set of the closed lips is neither downcast nor smiling; the straight accent line, however, extends the upper lip line lending a somber impression. The tiny shape of the eyes is enhanced by spiral threaded eyes with jewel like effect such as is found on the early SFBJ character dolls described in Chapter IV. The French body appearing on the doll may not be original, but is intriguingly correlated to these eyes and the mystery attribution. The German-French doll connection seems, again, exposed. Attributed to Simon and Halbig, marked III, 18", circa 1910.

Illustration 92.

Illustration 93.

Illustration 94.

Illustration 93. A facial view of the 1469 model by Simon and Halbig for Dressel.

Illustration 94. Production of the fashion doll model continued into the 20th century although facial and body modelling were indicative of changing aesthetics. The models shown here are of slightly later design than the Heubach model shown in Illustration 95, despite their at-first-glance similarities. Here the face, indubitably designed as adult, is daintily perched upon an elongated slender throat; yet the softness of diminutive facial features are almost childlike. The body is uniquely designed for the style: elongated torso, flattened bosom, tiny waist, slender and elongated limbs. The feet of one are designed for flat shoes while her partner has angled soles for higher- heeled shoes. In a slightly later variation the torso became even more boyish in dimension and the facial complexion bore a powdery matte finish; that model was designed as a flapper era fashion doll. Interestingly, both dolls shown here bear the model number 1469 although one is marked Simon and Halbig and the other COD for Dressel, circa 1915, 15".

Illustration 95, opposite page. The art character movement largely revolved around portraits of children. Except for depictions of historical figures, the designers rarely extended their creative inventory to include adult portraits. This demure, yet serenely poised, woman is thus a very rare example. Her cameo shaped face is turned just slightly sideways - a realistic gesture - and rests upon an elongated throat with well defined hollow. Unusually designed, the shoulderplate sides fit over the tops of the arms; the well-defined breasts are not illusory. Character is defined in the aquiline shape of nose, imperturbable smile and commanding posture. Gebruder Heubach, model 7926, 21". circa 1912.

Illustration 95.

Illustration 96. Variations in portrayal were achieved by structural as well as decorative variations. A smaller model of the fashion lady by Heubach, depicted in Illustration 95, is constructed as a socket head rather than shoulderhead and the mouth is modelled open with a tiny row of teeth rather than closed as in the larger example. The result is a more neutral gender; the doll would be suitable presented as either man or woman, while the larger model is decidedly female. Gebruder Heubach, 10", circa 1912.

Illustration 96.

Gebruder Heubach continued to produce a series of character dolls until well into the 1920's although all of the dolls bearing a four-digit model number were introduced by 1916. As the years ensued the extraordinary sculptural dimensions of the earlier examples diminished somewhat and were replaced by a reliance on mechanical gimmickry and caricature faces. Too, the company learned to compromise with economic reality; it was, after all, the appealing sleep-eyed child-doll that the public most demanded. Thus, during the latter part of the art character movement, the richly sculpted hair was replaced by malleable mohair wigs and the dimensional "intaglio" eyes were transfigured into sleeping glass eyes.

These second-period art character dolls by Gebruder Heubach are, justfully, sought by collectors. They evince remarkable personality despite their sometimes exaggerated expressions and, fairly, should be judged in their own right rather than in comparison to the earlier Heubach models. In all, the company produced in the short pre-war era a remarkable body of work.

Illustration 97.

Illustration 97. Introduced as "Whistling Jim", the Heubach character doll combined a unique sculpting of face with an effective, albeit primitive, body mechanism. Squeeze his torso and Jim will "whistle". The whistle was, in actuality, more of a squeek sound; it emitted through the "O" shaped hole in his mouth. The doll retains the deeply sculpted eyes of the earlier models although the sculpted detail of hair is barely defined. The modelling of the face is an effective enhancement to the mechanical action. Gebruder Heubach, 12", circa 1915.

The bandaged bull-dog was also created by Heubach and is an amusing precursor to the caricature dolls. Wonderfully expressive, his modelling extends to the folded wrinkles at back of neck; his scowling expression is more plaintive than fierce.

Illustration 98. Heubach continued to create children whose hair was adorned with ribbons and bonnets. These second-period dolls, however charming, lacked the masterful sculpting of the initial models. The blue-ribboned girl has an unusual downcast expression of eyes; the lids appear half-closed and are an effective counterpoint to a somber expression. Brightening the appearance is a high glaze decoration to the ribbon. The baby bonnet is ornamented with rich spiral designs overall the cap. Both Gebruder Heubach, 14" and 10", circa 1915.

Illustrations 99-102, opposite page. The masterful sculpting of the earlier period Heubach children metamorphosed into models of roguish imps. No subtle nuance of character here! What the art character doll now lacked in refinement, was supplanted by an appealing eccentricity. All four dolls by Gebruder Heubach, 8- 10", circa 1915.

Illustration 98.

Illustration 99.

Illustration 100.

Illustration 101.

Illustration 102.

Illustration 103. Although the sculpted hair and eyes of earlier Heubach children was replaced by "real" hair and glass eyes, the dolls continued to portray the "children of the streets". Wistful expressions with eyes half-closed in dreaminess or guilefully wide-awake were artfully achieved. The subtlety of complexion tones was enhanced by a rose tinting in the porcelain itself. The decoration was, at all times, understated; a simple wisp of tiny lashes, a single accent line between the delicate lips. Both Gebruder Heubach, 15", circa 1915.

Illustration 104, opposite page. It is a tenuous line between mere competence and art. Yet, curiously, the line is always evident as this blonde-haired doll portrays. The tiny eyes and full-formed lower cheeks and throat are, seemingly, contradictory. Yet they work. How simple seems the modelling of cheeks and mouth. Yet, upon reflection, one can see the detail of sculpting and decorative technique that combine to form a portrait of intense and thoughtful beauty. Gebruder Heubach, 18", circa 1915.

Illustration 103.

Illustration 104.

Illustration 105. A fascination with exotic cultures continued throughout the art character era. Unlike the pre-art-character dolls discussed in Chapter II, models were now designed to particularly portray ethnicity. In their registrations with the German courts, doll firms of the era made note of such descriptions as "Chinese", "Burmese", "Indian", "African", or "Eskimo", among others. In other instances, however, complexion tinting and decorative and costume illusions alone created the impression of ethnicity. Two models by Simon and Halbig, shown wigless for emphasis, illustrate this. The blue-gowned doll, model 1099 has unique sculpting specifically designed to depict an Oriental child; the illusion of Orientalness in the other model 1329 is simply a factor of her complexion and darkly painted brows. Yet both were created in the same era and, according to registration descriptions, both were designed as Oriental children. Both Simon and Halbig, 15", circa 1912.

Illustration 105.

Illustration 106. A pair of model 1099 Oriental children by Simon and Halbig illustrate the modelling variations that occur as a factor of size. The larger model has much more highly defined sculpting around the cheeks, mouth and eye corners. Simon and Halbig, 13" and 15", circa 1912.

Illustration 107, opposite page. The two Simon and Halbig Oriental dolls shown in Illustration 105 are shown here in full costume. It is evident that costume and headdress heighten the expression of ethnicity.

Illustration 106.

Illustration 107.

Illustration 108. Characterization was presented in various medium during the art-character movement. One alternative was celluloid which was popularized during this period. In this felicitous example, laughing faced babies, with variations in mouth and hair design, are compatible with the joyful bell- ringing they perform when the bellows mechanism is squeezed. Rheinische Gummi, circa 1912.

Illustration 109. During the hey-day of the art-character movement fantasy figure dolls were popular. Perhaps the most popular example of this was the googly-eye doll. The origin of this unusual design is arguable: was it inspired by such comic strip characters as Barney Google or was it an off-shoot of the Palmer Cox Brownie design or did the entire movement emanate from the popular magazine illustrations of Kewpie by Rose O"Neill? At any rate the movement was phenomenally successful. One popular example, shown here, was trademarked in America as the "Hug Me, Kiddies" doll. Constructed with mask composition face, the doll has impish over-sized googly eyes that are enhanced with equally unrealistic eyeshadow and brows that resemble nothing so much as a bruise half-healed, 13", circa 1912.

Illustration 108.

Illustration 109.

Illustration 110.

Illustration 110. It is difficult to imagine a design which more happily combines a fanciful waywardness with sentimental tug-of- the heart. It is, of course, the Kewpie, designed by the American artist Rose O'Neill. The artfulness of the little figure lies in its seeming simplicity. Yet all is harmony and balance in the perfectly composed design. Sculptural exclamations such as the peaked topknot add a sense of completeness to the design and are set apart by the smooth surrounding surface of the bald pate. Nothing is neglected in the design: the hair tumbles wonderfully from the little sprays; the nose, more an illusion than definition, allows prominence to the eyes as does the brows which are set, to the millimeter, a perfect distance from the eyes and perfectly capture the look of innocent impishness. One measure of the artfulness of the Kewpie design is its adaptability to variations as shown in this assortment of designs. Germany, all circa 1912.

Although Rose O'Neill had studied art professionally, had been designated a member of the prestigious Beaux Art Society in France, and left as legacy a body of serious art work including the infamous 'grotesque' paintings, it is for her design "Kewpie" that she will be mostly remembered. Of commercial origin - it first appeared in illustrative form in the pages of turn-of-the- century monthly women's magazines with a Kewpieville storyline also written by the artist - it quickly attained such popularity as to shadow - and overshadow - all other art work of the artist for the remainder of her life. Ironically, although Kewpie provided O'Neill with the financial security of which most artists only dream, it also became her nemesis. For years her time and creative energies were absorbed in over-seeing their development and production.

In other ways, the Kewpie was significant. A significant signpost of the blossoming American influence in doll design it was the first commercially important doll designed - and signed - by an American artist although produced in German porcelain firms. The movement foreshadowed a trend that would continue throughout the 1920's.

Illustration 111. One aspect of the artfulness of the Kewpie design was its adaptability. In this instance the Kewpie is created with glass eyes rather than painted. The eyes are heightened by thick black painted liner encircling the inner rim of the eyecut. The brows are heightened by raised modelling and glazed decoration; the detail of the hair is striking. Germany, Kestner, 16", circa 1912.

Illustration 112, opposite page. A village-ful of Kewpies was created by Rose O'Neill and many of the figures were identified and named. Although there is a family resemblance in each figure, there are also unique aspects of design. The googly eyes and blue wings of Doodledog indubitably mark its Kewpie relationship, yet the mouth is singularly designed; so is the case with black Kewpie known as Hottentot. Germany, circa 1912.

Illustration 111.

Illustration 112.

Illustration 113.

Illustration 114.

Illustration 115.

Illustration 113, opposite page. Kestner's impish googly bears a remarkable resemblance to Kewpie. Kestner, model 221, 10", circa 1910.

Illustration 114. Although patent and copyright infringement suits were an old story in the doll industry, the Kewpie may mark the first time an American artist held the copyright on her doll which was produced by another firm. O'Neill protected her design fiercely; yet she could not fully protect herself from companies that 'interpreted' her work. Beginning with the basic design they would change here, adapt there and a seemingly new doll was made. Kewpie could be marketed as "Cupie" and who would complain? In one instance, especially notable as it was made by Kestner who produced the actual copyrighted Kewpie shown in Illustration 111, a googly eyed imp bears a striking resemblance to Kewpie - even the body with the spread-open stubby fingers is similar. Yet enough differences occur to have protected Kestner from copyright suits: the painting of the brows, the more precisely defined and accented nostril, the shape of the mouth, the use of wig rather than uniquely painted Kewpie hair. Right, Kestner, model 221, 10", circa 1912. Left, O'Neill's Kewpie, 10", circa 1912.

Illustration 115. With smaller eyes, dainty nose, piquant smile and more realistically painted brows the googly became less a fantasy figure and more an appealing urchin. In this instance, the tender characterization is achieved by subtlety as opposed to the more radical expression of the Kestner googly model 221. Armand Marseille, model 241, 12", circa 1912.

Illustration 116. Another variation of the googly character shows the influence of the Kewpie design in the shape of the head and nose and in the modelling of curls onto the forehead and above the ears. Yet the design lacks the Kewpie topknot curl, has smaller eyes with variant decoration and a more widely smiling mouth. Hertel and Schwab, model 172, marketed as Jubilee Googly, 12", circa 1914.

Illustration 116.

Illustration 117. Kewpie design influenced the creation of other all-bisque googly style dolls. In most instances these googly figures were specifically targeted for the American market - they were created by American designers or they bore English language "pet names" that signified their destination. The two larger models, "Our Fairy" and "Baby Bud" continue the Kewpie-like theme with slight variations to ensure their singularity - the unique painting of feathered brows (curvy in the instance of Bud), the well defined mouths including delineation of tongue, the smaller eye cuts, and the wigged construction. The smallest doll is the most unique; its modelling includes unique design of tousled curly hair as well as body construction. The size of the iris of the googly eye is considerably diminished. The mouth is completely unique. Not coincidentally, the design also bears the imprimatur of a specific artist, the American illustrator Grace Drayton. All three models were introduced in 1914. 7" September Morn. 8" Baby Bud. 10" Our Fairy.

Illustration 117.

Illustration 118. In its purest sense the art-character doll reform movement in Germany lasted only a few years. Although artistically brilliant, the earlier character dolls never achieved the commercial success that would allow their continuity. The dollmakers could not continue their production. What should they do? Return to the non-characteristic dolly face model? This would not be a wise retreat either. Instead, the dollmakers compromised, creating and producing a series of character-like dolls with expressive and unique modelling which would, however, allowed the implementation of "real" teeth, sleeping eyes, and combable hair. The Kammer and Reinhardt model 117, known as Mein Liebling, was an instance of such a compromise as concerns the child doll. Now the dollmakers carried the compromise one step further in the introduction of the baby doll, then gaining popularity among children. Perhaps the most successful of these models introduced at this time was the trademarked "Hilda" baby. The doe-eyed gentle expression never fails to capture one's attention. Artful techniques used to attain this character expression include the extended modelling below the eyes, the over-glazed black highlights around the eyecut which give an illusion of tearfulness, the powdery soft rose complexion, and the unique and perfectly posed open lips. Kestner, model 237, Hilda, 12", circa 1914.

Illustration 119, opposite page. The on-going interest in exotic cultures took a new twist in this era. For the first time the exotic character was designed and created as a baby. The Oriental baby created by Kestner was a unique design; the model was used only for the production of the Oriental baby (later, in the 1920's Oriental babies would be produced by other firms but they were simply amber-tinted variations of stock baby models). The Kestner model was a superior work of art. It captured perfectly the characterization of the Chinese baby-toddler while avoiding stereotypical modelling and decoration. Its appeal was compelling while avoiding vapid sentimentality. Although the figure was specific in ethnicity and age, it was also universal in its humanness. Kestner, model 243, 14" and 20", circa 1914.

Illustration 118.

Illustration 119.

Illustration 120. Although the early 20th century art character doll has been attributed almost exclusively to the German schools, it is evident that a significant movement occured inFrance as well. The doll is described further in Illustration 127.

CHAPTER IV.

The Character Popularized French Dolls from the Early 20th Century

The art-character doll reform movement of Germany, 1905-1915, did not stop at the borders of France. Whether with philosophical intent or driven by economic considerations the French doll industry in the early 20th century also underwent a dramatic change in doll concept and production; the character doll was born.

Arguably, the art-character doll in France made a more dramatic appearance than it had in Germany. For certain, the German character doll had its antecedents in the pre-art characters as discussed in Chapter II. This had not been the case with the French doll; although a series of "character" heads had been created by Jumeau in the late 1880's they were so rare as to suggest their production exclusively for exhibition and automaton use. And while no one can deny that characterization was evident in the earlier French doll, this characterization was generally present "in spite of itself"; to these earlier French dollmakers attainment of beauty was a far worthier goal than delineation of character.

Illustration 121.

Illustration 121. French artists, such as the illustrator Francoise Poulbot, contributed to the design and creation of dolls during the French art character movement of 1905-1920. Within the French art community, however, Poulbot was more known for artwork such as this poster design than for his doll design.

After 1899 all this changed. Recognizing the waning popularity of their dolls, a number of prominent French dollmakers formed together into an organization named Societe Francaise de Bebes et Jouets or S.F.B.J. Their goal was to meet the German competition head-on. They would do this in two ways: first, by emulating German production and distribution procedures; and secondly, by creating a new style of doll suitable to the temper of this fledgling 20th century. Monsieur Baudy, director of the Manufacture Nationale de Sevres in 1962 noted, "At this time, 1915-1916...our archives...record that a small number of doll heads, modelled after certain heads of children of the 18th-19th centuries were made in our workshop in 1917/1918 as experiments.

Max Von Boehn, in his classic work, ***Dolls and Puppets***, written in the 1920's, called this movement the "Renaissance of the French Doll" and defined it as the "transference of attention from the elegant fashionable lady to the simple child".[1]

It is, again, the "child of the street" theme that surfaces. Playful urchin, insouciant imp, budding young child-woman, sensitive lad were all portrayed in a series of child portraits. In 1902 French firms offered a prize for the creation of character doll sculptures; renown artists such as the sculptor Fremiet and painters Detaille and Gerome competed for awards, although no particular doll design has ever been attributed to them. More known is the portrait of a young adolescent girl created by sculptor Albert Marque, the street urchin children of the French illustrator Francoise Poulbot, and the urchin children of the mysterious artist Van Rozen, although extant models of their works are so rare as to suggest their very limited production.

More commercially successful were a series of character dolls unattributed to specific artists. Produced as early as 1905, they continued to be created until the 1920's although it is unlikely that any new models were introduced after 1915-1916. This is the S.F.B.J. 200 series. Then during the 1920's this art character doll evolved into the studio doll, a product more specifically targeted for an adult art market than for children's play.

Although the early 20th century art character doll has been attributed almost exclusively to the German schools, it is evident that a significant movement occurred in France as well.

1. *The term "Renaissance of the French Doll" was actually coined by Monsieur Goin in article written about the Marque doll in 1916.*

Illustration 122. Although noted French artists contributed to the design of the French art character doll, the majority of character dolls produced during the early 20th century are unattributed to specific artists. Marked by a 3-digit serial number from the 200 series, the S.F.B.J. models have characteristic decoration of features such as an unusual brown painted eye lash with bi-level delineation of the upper lash. In the earlier examples, generally depicting older children rather than babies or toddlers, the face is slender, the complexion delicately colored, and the tiny eyes created with a brilliantly piercing jewel-like effect. The appearance is playful, yet gentle and sensitive. French, S.F.B.J. model 235, 16", circa 1910.

Illustration 122.

Illustration 123. The fretful faced child is the beneficiary of extraordinary modelling, although the sculptor is unknown. Lacking nuance in decoration, the model is more than compensated with artful composition of design: the perfectly sized and slightly squinting eyes are centered by the downcast lips and softly rounded nose. The delicate chin is perfectly appropriate to the age of the child depicted; the frown lines around the mouth are realistic. In the S.F.B.J. models which depicted young toddlers or babies, the sleep eye was utilized rather than the "jewel" style eye. French, S.F.B.J. model 252, 10", circa 1912.

Illustration 124.

Illustration 124. Seen in profile the well-developed temples of the forehead are evident, the character defined by their furrowed expression.

Illustration 123.

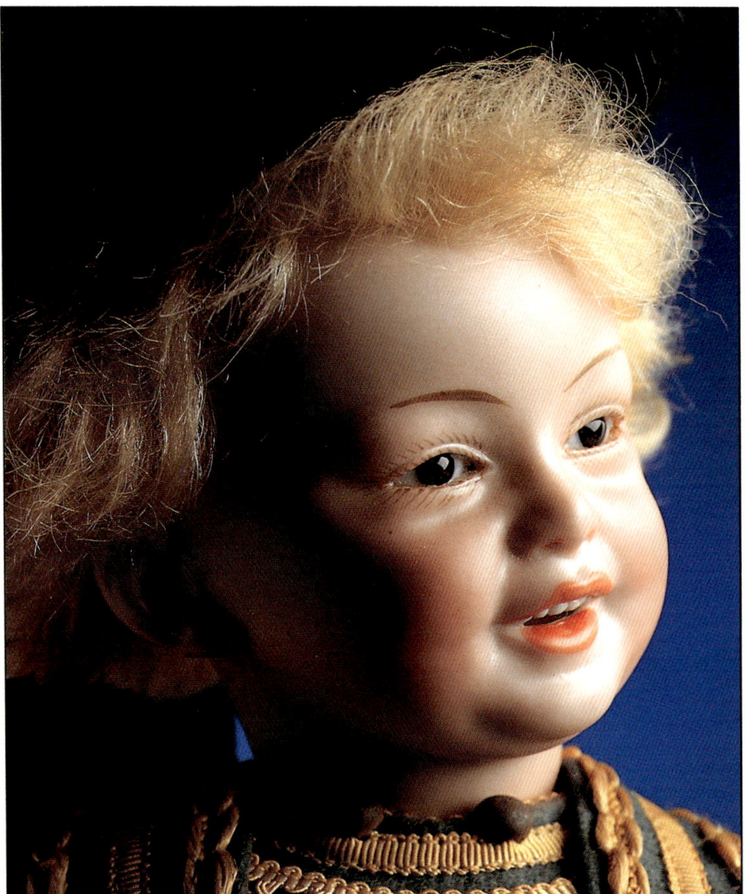

Illustration 125.

Another view of Illustration 125.

Illustrations 125-126. Two character models by S.F.B.J. are portrayed in a series of views. By examining the dolls from various perspectives the character portrayal is made more evident. Curiously, as with a real human face - and as in all good art - the dolls appear different when seen from various angles. Although the dolls are different models it is evident that there is strong familial unity. S.F.B.J. achieved variations with slight modifications of sculpture such as open or closed mouth, painted or wigged hair, and sometimes, as seen here, with an applied "fleeced" hair over sculpted hair base. French S.F.B.J. 229, 15", circa 1910. French S.F.B.J., 237, 13", circa 1910.

Illustration 126.

Another view of Illustration 126.

Illustration 127. The French character doll movement, as exemplified in the S.F.B.J. doll, gradually evolved into the baby or young toddler model. The face became rounder, more baby-like, the eyes wider and with sleeping mechanism, the mouth a near exaggeration of dimples and laughter lines. Although lacking the nuance of the earlier character models by S.F.B.J. the doll is exuberant and vital. A precursor to the copiously produced 236 model, this 234 model bears strong family resemblance, yet is indubitably its own person. French, S.F.B.J., model 234, 15", circa 1915.

Illustration 127.

Chapter V.

The Character in Evolution German Dolls, 1915-1925

Illustration 128. By 1914 the art reform character doll had already begun to be transformed. Features were softened, wigs and sleeping eyes - sometimes even flirting eyes - were added.

Illustration 128.

The doll art reform movement was dealt a serious blow by world events of 1915-1918. Certainly the embargo on German goods to America during this time had no small impact on the development of the American doll industry. It is curious how many American-made dolls from this era so closely resemble the German counterparts that were no longer available - the pouty-faced child by Schoenhut and the dolls by Horsman and Effanbee that were often virtually identical to models by Gebruder Heubach are examples.

Yet the more significant evolution that occurred in the doll world was not directly an effect of world events. After a few splendid years, it became obvious that the 'children of the street' models of the art reform movement were not commercially viable. It is difficult for us to conceive of that today, so magnificent do these dolls of 1909-1914 seem. Yet they simply did not sell in the quantities that the manufacturers deemed necessary. By 1914 the art reform character doll had already begun to be transformed. Features were softened, wigs and sleeping eyes - sometimes even flirting eyes - were added. The introduction of the model 117 by Kammer and Reinhardt, shown in the previous chapter, is perhaps most symbolic of that transformation. In other instances modifications were made to existing models - glass sleeping eyes were added to the 100, 101 and 114 models by Kammer and Reinhardt, for example. This trend continued and grew throughout the 1915-1925 era.

Conversely, another trend was developing. The classic German dolly-faced model - at its best, lovely and endearing; at its worst, vacuous - began to take on character. Manufacturers found that the addition of simple features - sculptural shaping and decorative highlights to lips or impressed dimples and laughter lines around eyes and mouth, for example - could render the doll more artful and give it a personality more appealing to children.

The character baby - often, an infant - achieved its apex during this period. The trend had begun with the popularity of such models as Hilda, discussed in the previous chapter, and now came to full fruition. Most symbolic of this trend was the Bye-lo Baby. A keystone in doll history by any standard, the doll enjoyed an immense popularity which earned it the dubious sobriquet "The Million Dollar Baby".

Designed by an American artist, Grace Storey Putnam, the doll was only one of a dozen or more successful designs created by American studio artists during this period and produced in German porcelain firms. This phenomenon was made possible by the strong American doll and toy distributor firms that had developed over the previous fifty years. With immense control over the largest doll and toy market in the world - America - and sometimes now even manufacturers in their own right, the distributor firms such as Horsman and Borgfeldt were in a position to make demands upon their German suppliers. Thus, during the 1920's the growth occurred of dolls which were designed and copyrighted by a named artist, (usually American) controlled and distributed by an American firm, and produced, under special commission, in German porcelain firms. These artists included Putnam, Jeanne Orsini, Georgene Averill, Helen Jensen, Joseph Kallus, and Charles Twelvetrees. Some, including Averill and Kallus, moved on in the next decade into the establishment of their own doll firms.[1]

"....Thus, during the 1920's the growth occurred of dolls which were designed and copyrighted by a named artist, (usually American) controlled and distributed by an American firm, and produced, under special commission, in German porcelain firms...."

It is curious that during this period the German firms did not initiate strong efforts in the development of new medium. It must have been obvious that such American dolls as Horsman's Can't Break'Em compositions and Schoenhut's woodens (advertised as indestructible) were finding a strong response in thrift-minded parents who were tired of replacing porcelain-headed dolls. It seems especially curious since the German toy industry had really 'invented' composition or paper-mache in the previous century. Yet by the time their efforts in this direction were concentrated it was too late. Although the German doll industry produced some delightful character dolls of composition throughout the 1930's they were little known or distributed beyond their own borders.

1. In a fitting historical irony, Kallus, a remarkable doll artist himself, later became the distributor of the O'Neill Kewpie doll which had begun the entire 'named-artist' movement.

Illustration 129. The character doll of the art reform movement, 1905-1915, was modified to make the doll more playful and appealing to children. The addition of wig, glass eyes and teeth to models that had originally appeared with painted hair and eyes and closed mouth was one method in which this was achieved. It should be remembered, however, that the transition was not a lengthy one; often, in fact, the original and transformed models were produced concurrently for a period of time. Boy, Germany, bisque model 161, Kley and Hahn, 13". Girl, Germany, bisque, model 604, Bahr and Proschild, 13". Both circa 1912.

Illustration 129.

Illustration 130.

Illustration 130. The modified character doll retained many of its original features. Deeply defined modelling around the eyes and mouth lent a realistic expression. Original costumes, such as this model enjoys, were not constructed for durability, but did initially serve to enhance the character portrayal. Germany, bisque, Bahr and Proschild, model 604, 13", circa 1912.

Illustration 132.

Illustration 131. Body style could also be used to define characterization. The toddler body, first developed during the art reform movement, gained new popularity now. It was especially effective to portray young children poised between infancy and school-age. One variation of the toddler body was the impish model shown here which had been strongly influenced by the O'Neill designed Kewpie body. The playful pose allowed by the body shape and articulation enhances the impish facial expression. Bisque, Germany, model 260, Kestner, 10", circa 1920.

Illustration 132. Although lacking the well-defined modelling of its art reform predecessors, the tiny-eyed doll surely expresses character. This is achieved through the tiny, yet expressive eyes with complementary decoration, and slightly open "O" shaped mouth. Bisque, Germany, model 233, Marseille, 12", circa 1920.

Illustration 131.

Illustration 133.

Illustration 133. The Schoenau and Hoffmeister firm came somewhat late to character dolls. In fact, in a curious twist of irony, their most famous doll was the portrait of England's Princess Elizabeth which was not introduced until after 1930. This model appeared long after the German character doll movement, and coincides more closely with the American celebrity doll movement discussed in Chapter Six. The doll shown here combines several features of the German post-art-reform movement. It capitalizes upon the popularity of the young toddler baby model, it utilizes character features such as wide eyes and baby over-bite while still retaining an appealing playfulness through glass eyes, teeth and wig. Bisque, Germany, Schoneau and Hoffmeister, Ox model, 16", circa 1920.

Illustration 134.

Illustration 134. Interest in ethnicity in dolls, begun in the 19th century and fully developed during the art-reform movement, continued into this era. Yet it was altered as this model shows. Although the eyes are specifically modelled to achieve an Oriental look, most of the characterization occurs through decoration of complexion and features, much as in the 1880-1905 era in Germany. Additionally, however, the strong interest in baby dolls had impacted - the doll is clearly an Eastern cousin to the Western Dream Baby, both, in fact, produced by the same firm. Bisque, Germany, Armand Marseille, 13" head circ., circa 1925.

Illustration 136.

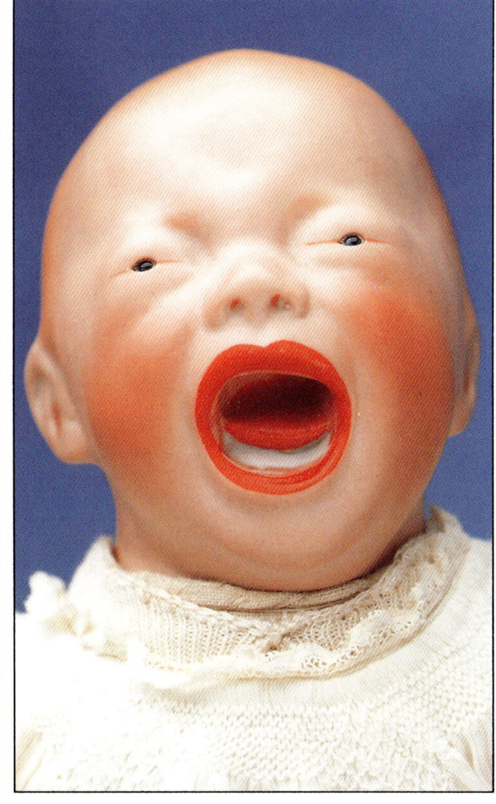

Illustration 135.

Illustration 135. Anomalies occur throughout doll history. This wailing baby, while borrowing upon the contemporary interest in infant dolls, is clearly in a position by itself. Elusively signed O.I.C - perhaps for an unknown artist - it remains a mystery why the doll was produced for surely it must have been lacking in appeal to the child. The character achievement is unique; while the eyes, for example, are of glass, they are so tiny as to be virtually undetectable. Bisque, Germany, marked OIC, 10" head circ., circa 1925.

Illustration 136. The character babies, introduced in the latter art reform movement era, gained new impetus during the 1920's. Now, however, special attention was made to the infant baby. Models were introduced with painted hair - just as in the art reform era - since this was the only way that the wispiness of newborn hair could be effectively presented. Sculptors paid special heed to the physiogomy of the newborn and in these models the delicate furrowing of corners around the tiny eyes is artfully achieved. In other instances the sculptors went so far as to delineate the unclosed skull-cap of the infant. Larger doll marked "Century Doll, Kestner", head circ. 12". Smaller doll marked Siegfried, head circ. 10". Both bisque, Germany, circa 1925

Illustration 137. The inspired sculpture, Bye-lo, of Grace Storey Putnam provided the model for many of the infant baby dolls of the 1920's. The original wax model by this American artist evolved into her porcelain dolls whose German production was under her complete control. So dominant was the doll that it was produced in a myriad of sizes and variations, as shown here, yet it was the original cloth-bodied baby that remained the most popular, and arguably, the most artful. This attention to body sculpting had not been wide-spread in the industry since the era of the 19th century French doll-makers. True, the Germans had continued to introduce new body styles and techniques, yet with the notable exceptions of O'Neill, Kruse, Marque, Poulbot and character dolls 123 and 124 (Max and Moritz) by Kammer and Reinhardt, no French or German dolls of the 20th century were designed with a unique body specifically designed to enhance the overall projection of character. So important did Storey consider her body design that she insisted that each body be signed for copyright protection. Various models of Bye-lo Baby, bisque, Germany, circa 1923.

Illustration 137.

Illustration 138.

Illustration 139.

Illustration 139A.

Illustration 138. The New York studio artist, Jeanne Orsini, created a small group of miniature doll designs during the late 1920's that were produced in German porcelain firms. With wonderfully exaggerated, yet appealing, features that accurately reflected the modern child, the dolls could fairly be labelled "children of the streets of the 1920's". Their slender-modelled torsos and elongated limbs were a pre-cursor to the soon-to-appear American composition play-doll of the 1930's. Each bisque, Germany, marked J.1.O., 5", circa 1927.

Illustration 139. In the design of the Bye-lo Baby, the artist Grace Storey Putnam was concerned with the production of the body as well as the head. In its most prolific form the doll was produced with a soft body made to simulate the shape, feel and weight of a real baby. In the all-bisque models many variations were produced in an attempt to compromise economical realities with the artist's original concept. For instance, a model was made with real hair and movable glass eyes.

Illustration 139A. The doll as infant baby was a highly developed character of the 1920's. Undoubtedly the commercial success of the Bye-lo influenced the production of similar designs, yet despite their sisterhood the artful examples of these dolls, like all good art, maintained their uniqueness. (See Illustration 137 for description.)

Illustration 140.

Illustration 141.

Illustration 140. Registering the tradename "Just Me" for this 1920's era impish child, the German firm of Armand Marseille obviously intended the doll for the American market. The "who me?" O-shaped eyes along with bow-shaped mouth design were certainly emblematic of the era and fairly depicted the popular concept of the contemporary child. 10",Marseille, circa 1927.

Illustration 141. In its original version, Just Me, was produced in the traditional painted and fired bisque. A few years later the painted finish was no longer being fired and the complexion tones became more highly exaggerated. During its later years, Just Me was bought, uncostumed, by Jennie Graves of the American doll firm, Vogue (who later produced Ginny) and costumed by her in contemporary little girl costumes of the early 1930's (as shown here in the model on the right). Just Me was surely a prototype of the modern child, and can be seen as a significant influence on 1930's era American dolls such as Patsy. The doll is a fitting symbolic bridge between German and American doll dominance during that 1920 and 1930 era. Each 10".

CHAPTER VI.

The Character as Personality American Dolls, 1925-1935

Illustration 142.

Illustration 142. Today's collectors recognize the persona of Charlie McCarthy, but perhaps tomorrow's collectors, no longer knowing the 'name' of the doll, will acknowledge the accurate portrait of the foppish gentleman. Effanbee, 20", circa 1937.

It is difficult for collectors to conceive of dolls from this era as being models of great art or as having character qualities. That is partly the result of modernity - we are, in a sense, too close to the dolls to judge them dispassionately and we wrongly judge that if a doll evinces our nostalgia it cannot be artistic as well. It is partly a result of new materials from which dolls were being made; the traditional porcelain was largely abandoned in favor of 'composition' materials which collectors, even today, tend to judge as 'less serious' artistically.

The situation is complicated by a another phenomenon which arose at this time. This was the development of the character celebrity doll. During the early 1930's American dollmakers, who had gained economic strength during the hiatus of German doll exportation from 1915-1918, introduced a series of dolls modelled after actual personalities - film stars, comic characters, heroes, media celebrities. It is true that 'portrait dolls' were not a distinctly new concept for during the 19th and early 20th century many German and French dolls had been modeled after celebrities such as Empress Eugenie, Jenny Lind, Buffalo Bill, and Admiral Dewey. But the American phenomenon took a distinctive twist - this was 'licensing'.

Under licensing agreements the celebrity (or original designer in the case of figures of imagination such as P.L. Crosby's Skippy) gave their permission to be sculpted and marketed as a doll. The licenses, costly arrangements, were closely guarded and eminently successful. This inspired the manufacturers to continue the creation of more and more licensed characters. Notable artists were commissioned to produce these models - a continuation of the 1920's movement when American artists such as Grace Storey Putnam and Georgene Averill had designed dolls that were produced in German porcelain firms. Considerable expense and effort was expended in the creation of superlative models.

The results were rewarding. Dolls of consummate characterization were designed and launched whose faces depicted the classical moods of children seen in earlier models. Pensive, impish, whimsical, somber, thoughtful, sensitive - all of these characterizations and more were portrayed in the character-as- celebrity dolls of the era. It is the failure of today's collector not to see beyond the celebrity nostalgia of these dolls in order to judge them as works of art, but it is a failure that time and fading memory will correct. Who *was* this person, we will wonder, and then, not remembering, will judge the doll on its ability to stand alone as model of character - or not.

Illustration 143. An older gentleman of kind and benign gentleness, tinged with an aura of smugness, is portrayed in this doll of the mid-1930's. Yet collectors, knowing the doll as Doctor Dafoe of Dionne Quintuplet fame, tend to judge it for nostalgia value rather than its characterization. American, Alexander, composition, 14", circa 1937.

Illustration 144. The eager, anticipatory expression of young childhood is ably portrayed in this model of a young toddler, no less than in its antecedent models from Germany and France. The doll was produced by the Averill Co. whose owner, Georgine Averill had designed the earlier Bonnie Babe made in German porcelain firm. American, composition, Snookums by Averill, 16", circa 1935.

Illustration 143.

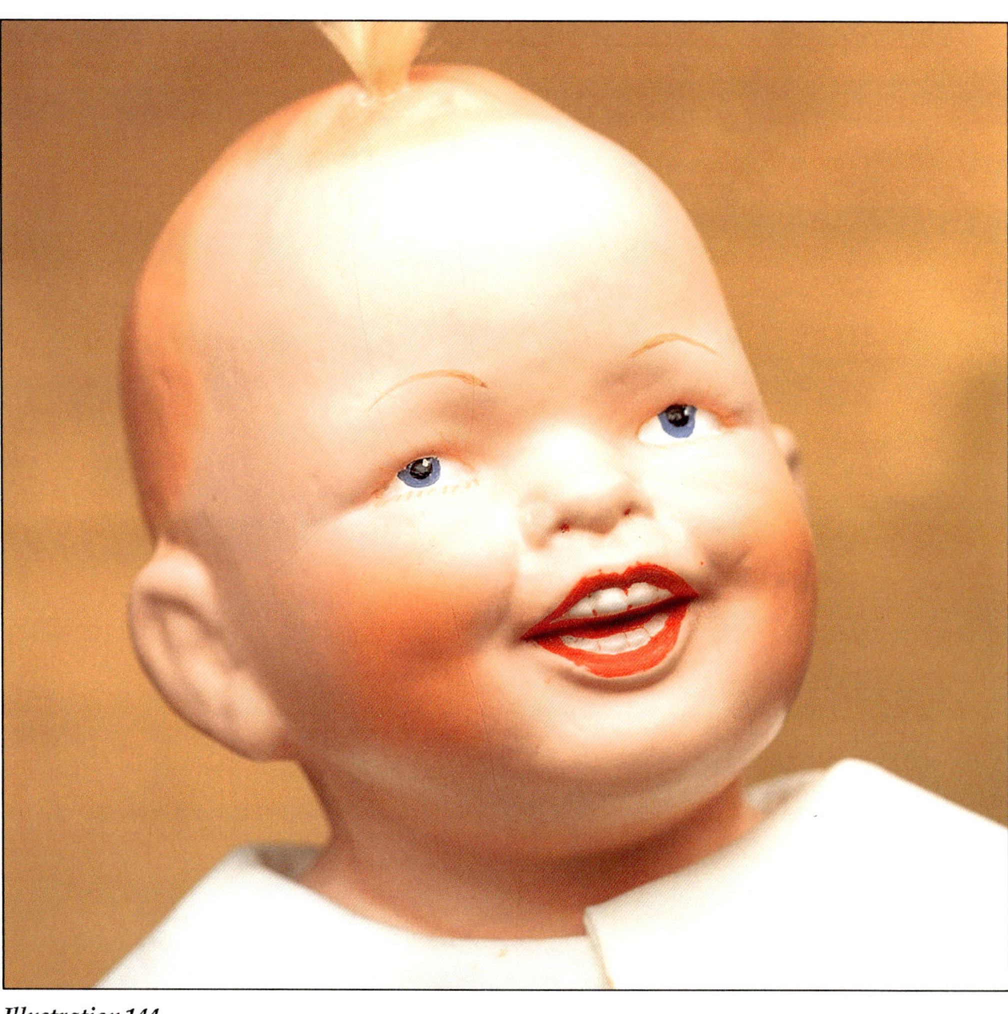

Illustration 144.

Illustration 145.

Illustration 145. Innocent impishness actuated from the tilt of the head, wide-eyedness with uplifted eyebrows, "O" shaped surprised mouth , posturing, and wispy tousled curls are wonderfully achieved in this 1930's model. However, the popularity of the doll, in its era and to collectors today, was a factor of its connection to an already popular figure, Skippy. Based upon the stories of Percy Crosby, the 'all-American boy' was re-created in the movies and again, re-created as a doll. Yet another judgment of the doll can be made that stands apart from its Skippy connection. That is simply the judgment that the doll is an apt and appealing portrait of a young child.American, Effanbee, composition, 14", circa 1935.

Illustration 146.

Illustration 146. Snappy and elegant, ultimately foppish, the gentleman aptly portrays a man of the world. Set in the 1930's and depicting a celebrity persona of that era, he nevertheless would be equally at home in a French court of the 18th century, so timeless are his features and personality. The portrait is enhanced by decorative accents of the face and costume. American, Effanbee, composition, portrait of Charlie McCarthy, 20", circa 1937.

Illustration 147. Snow White is characterizated as innocent and surprised. Yet even in this high production commercial doll character is achieved as a result of artistry in the original design.

Illustration 148, opposite page. The story of Snow White and the Seven Dwarves may prove to be timeless in itself, ensuring an ongoing interest in the dolls. Yet, even without this popularization, the portraits are worthy of exploration. Rather than simply creating a uniform mold with slight variations in decoration, the artist designed character features that emphatically portray the specific personality of each dwarf. The shape of the ear, the glance of the eyes, the shape of the mouth, for example, are characteristics that aid in defining each figure. Even without the celebrity status of these dolls, their character portrayal would be notable. American, Knickerbocher, Seven Dwarves, composition, 9", circa 1938.

Illustration 147.

Illustration 148.

Illustration 149.

Illustration 149. Successful dolls like all notable art, meet the aesthetic and moral requirements of their own era, but also convey universal and timeless qualities of person. An excellent example of this premise is the model trademarked as Patsy. Designed by the pre-eminent sculptor Bernard Lipfert, who also created the timeless model of Shirley Temple, the child was a prototype of the 1930's era child, yet still artfully conveyed the guileness sense of innocent mischief that has been a constant theme of character dolls from all eras. American, Effanbee, composition, Patsy, 9", circa 1935.

Illustration 150.

Illustration 150. Wearing his original costume, the doll is recognizable as Jackie Robinson to the 20th century student of social history. Yet lacking this specific identification the figure is still notable. Ethnicity is expertly portrayed in the doll in a manner that transcends the particular personality. American, Allied Grand Mfg., composition, 13", circa 1940.

Illustration 151. It is particularly appropriate that the Kewpie design by Rose O'Neill re-surfaces as the final selection of character dolls. Introduced shortly after the turn-of-the- century, the doll symbolizes several features that remained popular throughout the 20th century character doll movement. First is the characterization of fantasy figures, dolls that are human yet possessed of a metaphysical innocence that transcends the ordinary existence. Second is the realization of a doll from a pre-existing source - in this instance, the popular magazine stories of Kewpie by Rose O'Neill were the impetus to the creation of the doll. Third is the direct involvement of a notable artist in the design and production of the doll - Rose O'Neill remained concerned and involved with the production of her dolls throughout her lifetime. For O'Neill, as for her French forebearers of the previous century, it was the entire doll - the overall characterization - that was relevant. The stance of the body, the posturing, was as much a facet of character as were the facial features. Whatever the medium, age or nationality of a doll it is this constancy of purpose that defines a doll as character and as art. American, composition, Cameo, 12", circa 1935.

Illustration 151.

CHAPTER VII.

An Overview

In a sense, every doll attains its character from the instant it is placed in a child's hands. In the interaction between child and doll there is a tangible communication. The doll is characterized - made human - through the eyes and mind of the child and, to this purpose, it matters little whether the doll is the expensive masterpiece of an illustrious dollmaker or a crudely-stuffed old sock.

Yet *In Character* has sought to illuminate the ways in which dollmakers have moved beyond the primitive child/doll communion to instill in their dolls a specific characterization. So directed has this goal been at times that the dollmakers' purpose could be described as 'breathing life into the doll'.

Throughout *In Character* certain themes have surfaced again and again.

* As with all good art, the finest dolls portray a universality and timelessness. Despite their connection to a specific time and place in history they evince a humanity that transcends the specific. A thousand years later on the other side of the world they would 'speak' a common language to the viewer.

* Yet each character doll is also a product of its specific time and place, reflecting, for instance, particular concepts of beauty, of psychology, of artistic themes. Further, the character doll is not only affected by these larger societal issues but also by interconnections within the doll world - what one dollmaker has found successful has soon become the by-word of the whole industry. More practically, each doll is also a captive of the manufacturing possibilities of its time or place - the particular type of porcelain materials available to a dollmaker in America in 1875, for example, would certainly affect the type of doll created there.

* The history of characterization in dolls is evolutionary. Particular trends do not stand isolated in point of time or place but like all historical movements slowly transmute. The fashion doll - portraying sophistication and elegance - was not particular to France in the 1870's, for example, but has been a constant throughout doll history. Only the model has evolved as societal definitions of sophistication and elegance have evolved. The art character doll, popularly perceived as a specific product of Germany in the early 1900's, was not limited to the geographical limits of Germany nor was it circumscribed by its particular era. While it is true that certain movements achieved momentum or even crescendo in a particular time and place they invariably have roots in earlier movements and continuum in later ones.

The book, *In Character*, is the image of characterization in dolls as seen through the eyes of one collector, and is necessarily bordered by the scope of that collection. Other remarkable dolls which can further illuminate this concept of characterization, joyfully await the discovery of each new collector.

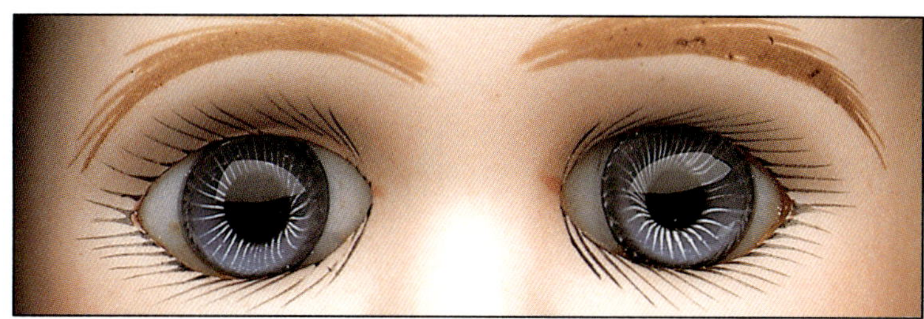

Illustration 152.

Illustrations 152 and 153. That the eyes are the mirror of the soul could be said to be a constant truism of doll-makers. In the earlier years, the French dollmakers sought to achieve a lifelike quality in the eyes, the depth and color being so real as to truly achieve a human quality. During the decade of the 1930's the attainment of characterization through the eyes is a bit more artificial or forced, yet the desired goal was also achieved. Through painted detail - amazingly simple in examples such as Illustration 153 - entire characterizations could be achieved.

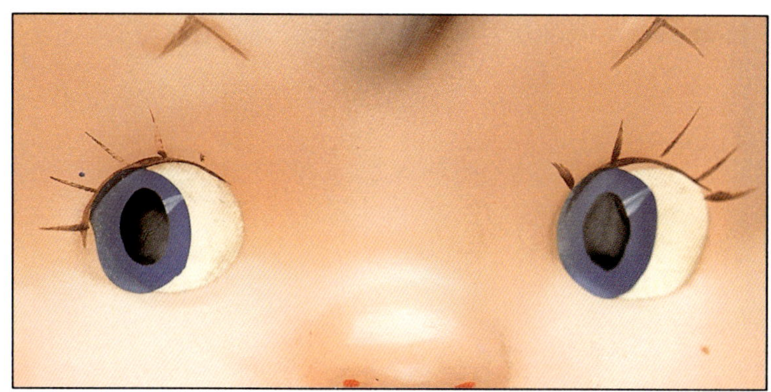

Illustration 153.

Illustrations 154 and 155. Within the same era, certain treatments of facial characteristics often bore remarkable similarities. Shown above are eye treatments on Grace Drayton's model trademarked as September Morn and Kestner's 221 model. The eyes are virtually identical in shape, glance and decoration.

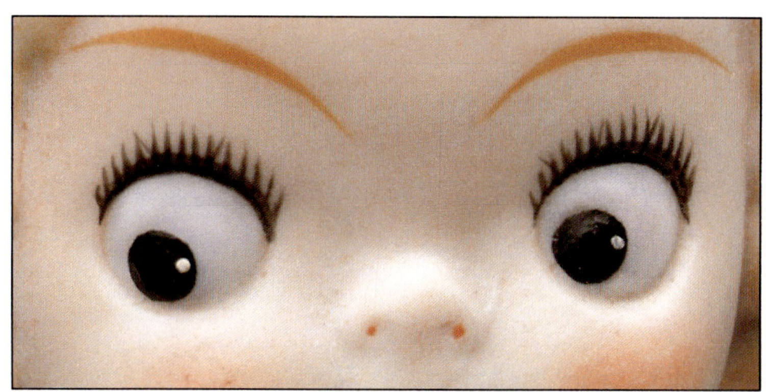

Illustration 154.

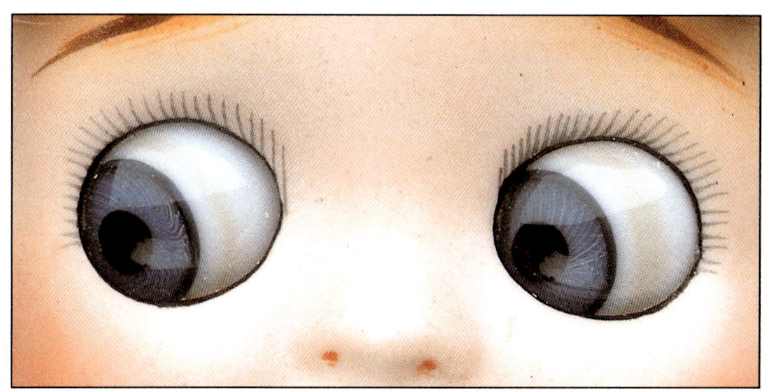

Illustration 155.

Illustrations 156, 157, 158 and 159 (shown here and on opposite page). Characterization concerned itself not only with portrayals of children but with that of adults as well. Further the portrayals of adult included various ethnic groups as well as historical and fantastical figures. Shown here and opposite are four examples of adult characters produced during the 20th century. A close-up of George Washington, shown in Illustration 156, depicts a stern-faced figure somewhat more youthful than he was frequently depicted in 18th century portraits. He is, nonetheless, indubitably George Washington. Interestingly, the model appears to be unique to this figure while, for example, other adult portraits were re-fashioned by changes in decoration, costume and coiffure, and - presto - were transformed into someone else. The Uncle Sam model by Dressel, for example, also appeared as an aged farmer and Dressel 's Hexe model was variously decorated to become Old Rip. The gaunt-faced aged Indian of Gebruder Heubach was produced invariant form as an Eskimo and as either male or female.

Illustration 156.

Illustration 157.

Illustration 158.

Illustration 158. The caricature face shown in Illustration 158 is indubitably that of an adult man yet the model draws freely from popular childhood themes of its turn-of-the-century era such as googly eyes. Curiously, a remarkable similarity exists between this gnome-like model and the funny-featured Seven Dwarves modelled some thirty years later.

Illustration 159. The aged gentleman, also shown in Illustration 143, verges upon the sentimentally maudlin. Yet in spite of the overt utter sweetness another quality of righteous smugness emerges. The total 'character' of the figure is evident to all.

Illustration 159.

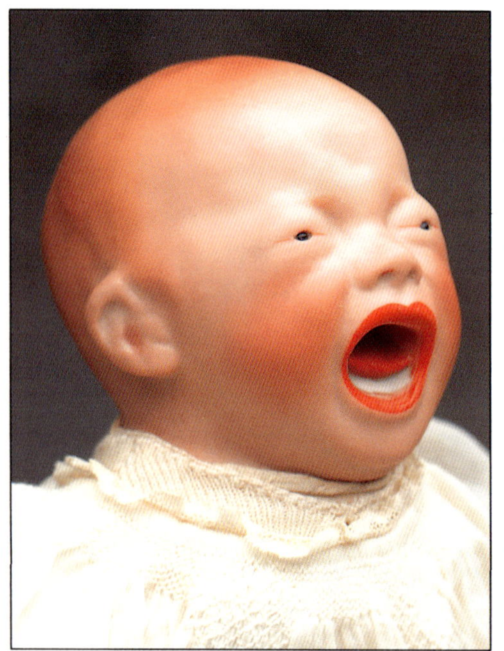

Illustration 160.

Illustrations 160 and 161. It is remarkable how certain moods of childhood emerge over and over again in doll models. The wailing character children shown above were designed during the first quarter of the 20th century, yet they were preceded by a very similar model by Emile Jumeau made about 1880 and followed by various composition and, later, plastic models including a composition doll by Georgene Averill and Bi-Bye Baby by Beverly Dolls.. However, in each of the models there were variations in styling and decoration - the OIC baby (top) is more highly colored and the eyes are tiny embedded glass, while the Heubach boy (bottom) has a wonderfully textured complexion that enhances the sorrowing expression and the eyes are sculptured and painted rather than glass.

Illustration 162 (opposite page). Ethnicity in character dolls, if not prevailing, was a significant secondary trend throughout the 1875-1935 era. Ethnicity was expressed in one of two general ways: most commonly, stock doll models were decorated and costumed to represent one or another ethnic group; in rarer examples, dolls were precisely modelled with correct physiogomy. In the group of Oriental dolls, made in France and Germany, 1880- 1925, shown on the opposite page these variations are well expressed.

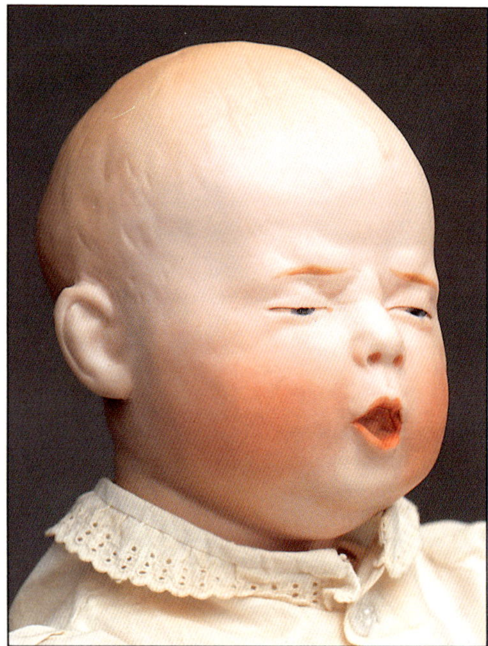

Illustration 161.

Illustration 162.

Illustration 163. Characterization in the doll was achieved through facial modelling, body construction, posture and costume.

Illustration 164.

Illustration 164. Vogue-ish theories of social reform and education are reflected in the models of dolls created at a particular time, yet are never wholly isolated in time and place from similar dolls. The 'art reform' character dolls of early 20th century evolved over several earlier decades, just as did the social and educational precepts which influenced their creation.

Illustration 165. That dolls from differing eras and places can be successfully intermingled illuminates their artistic universality.

Illustration 166.

Illustration 166. Characterization in dolls was achieved not only through facial sculpting, but also through the entire product. Ability to pose and articulate the doll in a realistic, human-like manner was an important factor not only of play but also of art.

Illustration 167. Yet each doll was also a product of its particular moment in history. The French bebes lend themselves more to the 'parlour play' deemed suitable for young ladies of the Victorian era while the German children seen in Illustration 164 are, indubitably, 'children of the street'.

Illustration 167.

Illustration 168. In the finest doll creations, the moods and expressions of childhood are perfectly portrayed. These expressions transcend any particular time and place and are truly 'in character'.

Index Of Doll Makers

Allied Grand 114

Bahr and Proschild 60, 100, 101

Barrois 16

Bru, Leon Casimir 14, 18, 19

Cameo 115

Effanbee 109, 111, 114

Gaultier, F. 20, 40

Hertel and Schwab 88

Heubach, Gebruder 61-66, 72-79, 98, 118, 120

Jumeau, Emile 16, 20-37, 44

Kammer and Reinhardt 50, 52, 53, 54, 55, 68, 69, 70, 90

Kestner 42, 46, 48, 51, 59, 60, 87, 90, 91, 102, 105, 117

Kley and Hahn 51, 100

Knickerbocker 112, 113

Kruse, Kathe 51, 68

Kuhnlenz, Gebruder 43

Marseille, Armand 68, 87, 102, 104, 108

May Freres 40

Rabery and Delphieu 40

Rheinische Gummi 51, 82

Schmitt et Fils 20

Schoenau and Hoffmeister 103

S.F.B.J. 92-97

Simon and Halbig 44, 46, 49, 56, 57, 58, 59, 69, 70, 71, 72, 80, 81

Steiff, Marguerite 51

Steiner, Jules 38